The
GAME
and
FISH
MENU
COOKBOOK

Also by Timothy Manion

WILD GAME AND COUNTRY COOKING
AMERICAN HUNTING & FISHING GUIDE

The
GAME
and
FISH
MENU
COOKBOOK

A Country Collection

Timothy E. Manion

Illustrated by Sharon Anderson

Weidenfeld & Nicolson
New York

Published by Weidenfeld & Nicolson, New York
A Division of Wheatland Corporation
10 East 53rd Street
New York, NY 10022

Library of Congress Cataloging-in-Publication Data
Manion, Timothy.
The game and fish menu cookbook.
Includes index.
1. Cookery (Fish) 2. Cookery (Game) I. Title.
TX747.M255 1987   641.6′92   86-28111
ISBN 1-55584-127-9
ISBN 1-55584-061-2 (pbk.)

Manufactured in the United States of America

Designed by Irving Perkins Associates

First Edition

10 9 8 7 6 5 4 3 2

To my family:
Melody,
Mother, Father,
Barbara, Rick, Dennis,
Barton, John,
and Radar the Wonder Dog.

CONTENTS

❦

INTRODUCTION

Like most hunting and fishing enthusiasts, I can easily recollect my early years of learning about the outdoors and can still feel the pride I had in bringing home game for the first time. However, unlike most hunting and fishing enthusiasts, I also learned to cook the wildlife I caught.

After graduation from college (with a degree in hotel and restaurant administration), I found my interests greatly changed. I still loved to fish and hunt, but the complete joy was in preparing a gourmet meal with the result of a successful expedition. I began to experiment with new flavors and to find ways to dispel old wives' tales. I was determined to find a use for everything in our overstocked freezer, full of fish and game. So my future was set—I would enjoy the outdoors and be equally enthusiastic in the kitchen.

Hunting, cooking, and eating game is central to our American culinary heritage. The richness of the land gave a natural advantage to our pioneering forebearers. Hunting and fishing for food was as expected as cutting wood for the fire. Although life today is vastly different than it was two hundred years ago, many Americans still enjoy hunting and fishing for food, as I do.

Most hunters and fishermen are also, in their own way, expert environmentalists. Sound and sensible conservation allows the fish and game population to remain stable (and in most areas, increase). Public awareness has helped ensure that the environment will be safe for both man and wildlife. With this concern, most outdoorsmen take and keep only what they can use. More are learning that cooking a fine dinner for friends, and sharing with them tales of the last hunting or fishing trip, are thrills equal to the catch itself.

In *The Game and Fish Menu Cookbook*, I have attempted to remove the mystique from wildlife cooking. You can expand your game and fish repertoire and no longer have to schedule that extraordinary venison or luscious goose dinner only for a special occasion. This is as it should be, since fish and game are good for you and should be eaten frequently. They are high in nutrition and low in saturated fats, cholesterol, and calories.

There is absolutely nothing to compare with the sweet taste of freshly caught, beautifully prepared fish. Whether saltwater or fresh, each will have a distinguishing flavor that cannot be duplicated. Certainly, any fish dish is a welcome meal for dieters, people on restricted diets, or for those simply concerned with good eating and health habits. Poached or steamed, served with a hint of citrus and a bit of dill, fresh fish is a pure delight.

In order to produce a meal that will have guests raving, it is important to control every aspect of the handling of game, from the time it is shot and transported, to its storage and preparation. Deer, moose, antelope, or bear, each has its own distinctive flavor and taste. Some call this "wild and gamey," but I prefer to use the term "richness." Many say they cannot tell the difference in the varying tastes of big game. However, when game is properly prepared and handled, the flavor of each will be defined and clear.

Americans more and more are discovering what Europeans have known for centuries: venison is delicious. The flavor and taste of this fine-textured meat is a direct result of the animal's diet, the conditions under which it is shot, and how it is handled, stored, and prepared. Venison's distinctive flavor is being enthusiastically enjoyed across the country; in Wisconsin alone over 22,500,000 pounds of the meat was processed in 1986. It is, therefore, good practice to either take the deer yourself or to know the hunter. I have used the category "venison" to include other big game such as moose, elk, and antelope.

Hunting upland birds provides fast gunning as well as some of the best tasting table fare available from the wild. If I were to rate the most challenging species to hunt, surely the turkey would be revered as the king and the pheasant the prince of the wilds. "Upland birds" is for me an all-encompassing term when discussing turkey, pheasant, grouse, quail, dove, and chicken. The flavor of pheasant and grouse is distinctive and delicious on its own and does not always need to be embellished by heavy sauces. However, a light sauce enhanced with citrus or wine flavor will bring out the delicate flavor of the meat.

Duck hunters are a special breed. They will reach their hunting destination no matter what the weather or what they have to trudge through. In fact, for duck hunting, the worse the weather the better the waterfowler likes it. With the hard work involved in bagging the quarry, it is no wonder that many game cooks regard a well-prepared duck dinner as a real treat.

Introduction

Wild duck is smaller in size and has less fat than domestic duck. Since it is a migrating active flyer, more blood is pumped into the breast muscles to make them stronger, which results in a darker meat with a more robust flavor. The best eating are the puddle ducks (such as mallards, pintails, wood ducks, and blackduckers), since they feed on less fish and aquatic food than lake ducks (such as bluebills, red heads, or ruddy ducks).

I have designed the menus to complement the flavors of the featured fish or game. (And having a menu cookbook also eliminates the need to spread cookbooks about when you are confined to the stove!) I have tried to keep the recipes simple to prepare and easy to read, with the fish or game the featured attraction.

When recipes call for a particular fish or meat and you find it unavailable in your area, you may refer to my substitution chart for another selection. If you cannot locate the type native to your locale, ask your fish market or butcher for assistance. Do not hesitate to use recipes given for wild duck for domesticated and those for game for commercially available meats.

Tips on handling and storage will be found in a separate chapter. These have all been discussed on my television series, "Wild Game and Country Cooking," for use by the novice outdoorsperson-chef.

The Game and Fish Menu Cookbook is a chronicle of my years as a hunter-fisherman and game cook. The menus have evolved from trial and error; the tips from daily use. I hope through reading this cookbook you will develop a newfound excitement and appreciation for wild game cookery.

The
GAME
and
FISH
MENU
COOKBOOK

Chapter One

SHARON ANDERSON

FISH

MENU

❦

Friday Night Fish Fry

Cranberry Baked Beans

Tossed Spinach

Buttermilk Biscuits

Butter Pecan Tartlets

FRIDAY NIGHT FISH FRY

4 pounds walleye fillets (perch or panfish can be substituted)
1 cup saltine crumbs
3 eggs
¼ cup milk
¼ teaspoon pepper
  Salt to taste
¼ teaspoon onion powder
¼ teaspoon garlic powder
2 cups peanut oil
2 fresh lemons, cut into wedges

Butterfly fillets and pat dry on paper towels. Set aside. Place saltine crumbs in a dish. Whisk eggs, milk, pepper, salt, onion powder, and garlic powder together. Dip fillets in egg mixture, then cracker crumbs. Heat peanut oil, in a heavy skillet over high heat,

5

until smoking. Add fillets and deep fry for approximately 2 to 3 minutes, or until golden brown on each side. (Do not overcook.) Drain on paper towel. Serve hot with lemon wedges. *Serves 6.*

CRANBERRY BAKED BEANS

1½ cups dried beans
  2 cups cranberry juice
  2 cups water
  ⅓ cup chopped onions
  2 tablespoons molasses
  1 teaspoon dry mustard
  ⅛ teaspoon ginger
  ¼ cup catsup
  2 packed tablespoons dark brown sugar
1½ teaspoons salt
  ¼ pound salt pork, sliced

Wash beans and soak overnight in combined cranberry juice and water. Bring beans to a boil in the soaking liquid. Cover and lower heat. Simmer for about 3 hours or until beans are tender. If necessary, add more liquid to keep beans from sticking. When tender, drain and place in a large bowl; reserve the cooking liquid. Add onions, molasses, mustard, ginger, catsup, brown sugar, and salt, and mix well. Turn half the mixture into a bean pot. Arrange half the salt pork slices over the beans. Add remaining beans and top with remaining salt pork and reserved liquid. Cover and bake at 250°, for 6 to 8 hours or until beans are tender. Uncover for the last hour and add water if necessary to keep the beans from drying out. *Serves 6.*

TOSSED SPINACH

2 pounds spinach, thoroughly washed and trimmed of stems
1 bunch watercress, thoroughly washed and dried
½ cup chopped scallions
1 tablespoon fresh lemon juice
2 tablespoons olive oil
  Salt and pepper to taste

In a deep saucepan, bring approximately 4 quarts of water to a boil. Place spinach in a colander or sieve and quickly immerse in boiling water. You *do not* want to cook the spinach, just barely wilt it. Remove and rinse in cool water. Drain. Lightly toss spinach together with remaining ingredients. Serve at room temperature. *Serves 6.*

BUTTERMILK BISCUITS

2 cups all-purpose flour
1 teaspoon salt
½ teaspoon baking soda
1 teaspoon baking powder
3 tablespoons shortening or butter
¾ to 1 cup buttermilk

Preheat oven to 400°. Combine flour, salt, baking soda, and baking powder. Cut in shortening until mixture resembles coarse meal. Stir in enough buttermilk to make a soft dough. Turn onto a floured surface. Roll to ½-inch thickness, and cut out with floured biscuit cutter. Bake at 400° for 12 to 15 minutes or until biscuits are light brown. Serve immediately. *Makes 12 to 16 biscuits.*

BUTTER PECAN TARTLETS

½ cup butter
1 cup brown sugar
1 egg, beaten
½ cup pecans
1 recipe Plain Pastry

Preheat oven to 325°. Cream butter and sugar until fluffy. Add egg and mix thoroughly. Fold in pecans, broken into coarse pieces. Roll pastry thin and cut into 3-inch squares. Place the squares into small muffin pans, fitting them in so that the points are up, like the petals of a flower. Drop a tablespoon of the nut mixture into each cup and bake at 325° for 20 to 25 minutes or until set and light brown. *Makes 8 to 10 tartlets.*

PLAIN PASTRY

2 cups sifted flour
3/4 teaspoon salt
2/3 cup shortening
4 to 6 tablespoons ice-cold water

Sift flour and salt together. Cut in shortening with two knives or pastry blender. Add water, using only a small portion at a time, until mixture will hold together.

Divide pastry in two and roll out one half on a floured board. Line a 9-inch pie pan with the dough, trimming away the excess. Roll out the other half to top the filling, if you are making a two-crust pie. Or, cut the dough into sections as desired. If a baked crust is needed, prick the dough with a fork and weight it with dried beans or rice, then bake at 450° for approximately 15 minutes or until light brown. *Makes enough for one 2-crust pie, or approximately 2 dozen tarts.*

MENU

🐟

*Irene Guthrie's Fish Creole
with Rice*

Endive and Apple Salad

Southern Fritters

Frozen Strawberry Cake

IRENE GUTHRIE'S FISH CREOLE

$\frac{1}{2}$ *pound cooked, flaked walleye*
$\frac{1}{4}$ *cup butter*
 2 *teaspoons chopped onion*
$\frac{2}{3}$ *cup chopped celery*
 2 *tablespoons chopped pepper, red and green*
$\frac{1}{4}$ *cup flour*
$2\frac{1}{2}$ *cups canned tomatoes*
$\frac{1}{3}$ *cup water*
 1 *bay leaf*
$\frac{1}{2}$ *teaspoon salt or to taste*

Melt butter in heavy skillet over medium heat. Add onion, celery, and peppers. Sauté for 5 minutes, stirring frequently. Blend in flour, tomatoes, and water. Stir until sauce boils and thickens.

9

Add fish, bay leaf, and salt. Cover and simmer over low heat, for 15 minutes. Remove bay leaf and serve over long-grain rice. *Serves 4.*

ENDIVE AND APPLE SALAD

4 medium heads Belgian endive
1 large red apple
1 teaspoon lemon juice
3/4 cup toasted walnut or pecan pieces
1 recipe Apple Dressing

Wash and trim endive. Separate leaves. Core and thinly slice apple. Sprinkle with 1 teaspoon lemon juice to keep slices from turning brown. Mix endive, apple, and nuts together. Toss with Apple Dressing and serve immediately. *Serves 4.*

APPLE DRESSING

1/2 cup walnut oil (or olive oil)
1/4 cup apple cider vinegar
3 tablespoons apple juice
1 teaspoon minced fresh chives
  Salt and pepper to taste

Whisk all ingredients together. Refrigerate, covered, until ready to use. *Serves 4.*

SOUTHERN FRITTERS

1 egg
1/2 cup milk
1 cup flour
1 teaspoon baking powder
1 teaspoon salt
1 teaspoon vegetable oil
1 12-ounce can Mexicorn
1 cup vegetable oil (more if needed)

Beat egg. Add remaining ingredients except 1 cup oil, stirring well after each addition. In a heavy skillet over high heat, bring oil to smoking. Drop batter by teaspoonful into fat. (Do not overcrowd pan.) Deep fry until golden brown. Remove from heat. Drain on paper towel. Serve hot, as is or with gravy or syrup. *Serves 4 to 6.*

FROZEN STRAWBERRY CAKE

1½ cups crushed strawberries
⅔ cup sugar
  1 tablespoon lemon juice
  3 cups graham cracker crumbs
½ cup heavy cream
1½ teaspoons vanilla
     Whipped cream, optional
     Fresh strawberries or pecan halves, optional

Combine all ingredients, except optional garnishes. Blend well. Line freezer tray with buttered parchment paper. Fill and freeze for approximately 2 hours, or until firm. Remove from freezer, unmold and cut into squares. Top each square with whipped cream, a fresh strawberry, or a pecan half, if desired. Serve immediately. *Serves 4 to 6.*

MENU
✿

Walleye Vera Cruz

Dried Corn Fritters

Sautéed Zucchini

Apple Brown Betty

WALLEYE VERA CRUZ

3 pounds walleye fillets
1 large onion, thinly sliced and separated into rings
3 cloves garlic, minced
3 tablespoons olive oil
2 cups stewed tomatoes
2 jalapeño peppers, seeded and sliced thin
1 small jar pimento-stuffed green olives, drained and sliced thin
¼ teaspoon ground cinnamon
  Pinch ground cloves
  Juice of ½ lemon
  Salt and pepper to taste
1 tablespoon capers, for garnish
  Cilantro leaves, chopped for garnish

12

Preheat oven to 350°. In a heavy skillet, over medium heat, sauté onions and garlic in olive oil until tender, but not brown. Add tomatoes, jalapeño peppers, olives, cinnamon, cloves, and lemon juice. Simmer over low heat approximately 5 minutes. Keep warm.

Place fish in a single layer in a greased shallow baking pan and bake at 350°, for about 15 minutes or until fish flakes easily. Arrange the fish on a heated platter and spoon sauce over the fish. Garnish with capers and cilantro. *Serves 6.*

DRIED CORN FRITTERS

2½ *cups milk*
2 *cups Pennsylvania Dutch dried corn*
2 *eggs*
1 *teaspoon sugar*
1 *teaspoon salt*
2 *teaspoons baking powder*
¾ *to 1 cup all-purpose flour*
 Vegetable oil for frying

Stir the milk into the dried corn and let stand for 45 minutes. Beat the eggs lightly and add to the corn and milk. Stir in sugar and salt. Mix baking powder with ½ cup flour and stir into the corn, adding enough additional flour to produce a stiff batter. Heat oil, covering a large skillet to ⅓ inch high, over high heat. Drop batter, by the tablespoonful, into the hot oil, and fry until golden brown on both sides, turning once. Remove from heat and drain on paper towel. Serve immediately. *Serves 6.*

SAUTÉED ZUCCHINI

4 *medium zucchini, grated*
2 *cloves garlic, minced*
½ *cup finely chopped onion*
½ *teaspoon grated fresh lemon peel*
¼ *cup olive oil*
 Salt and pepper to taste
¼ *cup grated cheese, optional*

Mix the zucchini, garlic, onion, and lemon peel together. Let set for about 15 minutes. Squeeze off all liquid. Pour olive oil into a heavy skillet. Bring to sizzle over medium heat. Toss in the zucchini, onion, and garlic. Sauté, stirring frequently, for about 5 minutes, or until zucchini has started to cook but is still crisp. Add salt and pepper to taste. Sprinkle with grated cheese. Serve immediately. *Serves 6.*

APPLE BROWN BETTY

6 cups peeled, cored, and thinly sliced McIntosh apples
3 cups coarse dry bread crumbs
1 cup dark brown sugar
⅓ cup molasses
3 tablespoons butter
½ teaspoon ground cinnamon
⅛ teaspoon ground cloves
½ cup hot water

Preheat oven to 350°. Butter a 2-quart pudding mold or glass baking dish. Arrange a layer of sliced apples on the bottom, cover with a cup of bread crumbs, sprinkle with ¼ cup sugar and 2 tablespoons molasses. Dot with 1 tablespoon butter.

Build alternate layers of apples and bread crumbs. Sprinkle with molasses and sugar and dot with butter. End with a layer of apples sprinkled with ¼ cup of sugar and the spices. Add the hot water, cover tightly with aluminum foil and bake for 35 to 40 minutes, or until top is richly browned and crusty. Remove from heat. Unmold and serve hot or warm. *Serves 6 to 8.*

OTHER RECIPES

❀

SHORE LUNCH WALLEYE

3 pounds dressed walleye, head removed
1 lemon, sliced
1 teaspoon salt
1 teaspoon dried tarragon leaves, or 2 teaspoons chopped fresh
  tarragon
1 teaspoon lemon pepper seasoning
1 teaspoon onion powder
  Lemon wedges, for garnish

Line fire bowl of covered grill with heavy-duty aluminum foil, and prepare coals for cooking. Lightly grease a sheet of foil large enough to wrap fish. Place three lemon slices on foil, top with fish. Combine seasonings and sprinkle on fish inside and out. Top with remaining lemon slices. Wrap in aluminum foil. Cook in covered grill over medium-hot direct heat 25 to 30 minutes, or until fish flakes easily with fork, turning packet over after 12 minutes. Garnish with fresh lemon. *Serves 2 to 3.*

FISH ITALIANO

1 5-pound walleye, cleaned
⅔ cup finely chopped onion
⅔ cup finely chopped carrot
⅔ cup finely chopped celery
  Several sprigs of parsley
  Sprig of thyme
1 bay leaf
2 cloves garlic, crushed
  Salt and pepper to taste
1½ cups red wine
½ cup water
3 tablespoons butter
3 tablespoons flour
  Juice of 1 lemon

15

Grease a Dutch oven. Add all vegetables, herbs, salt, pepper, wine, and water. Bring to a boil over medium heat. Place fish on the bed of vegetables, cover pan, and simmer for 18 minutes, or until fish is cooked.

While fish is cooking, melt the butter in a small saucepan, over low heat. Blend in the flour. Remove the fish to a hot platter and keep warm. Strain the fish liquid and add gradually to the butter and flour. Stir until thick. Taste for seasoning and add lemon juice. Pour over the fish and serve immediately. *Serves 4.*

BRAISED STUFFED NORTHERN PIKE

  1 5-pound pike
½ cup chopped onion
  4 tablespoons butter
½ pound ground smoked ham
  2 cups dry bread crumbs
½ cup chopped fresh parsley
½ teaspoon ground thyme
   Salt to taste
  1 teaspoon freshly ground pepper
  3 eggs
  4 tablespoons melted butter
   White wine
  3 strips salt pork
  2 tablespoons softened butter
  3 tablespoons flour
  2 egg yolks
  1 teaspoon lemon juice
¼ cup chopped fresh parsley

Preheat oven to 350°. Clean the fish and prepare for stuffing. In a heavy skillet, over medium heat, sauté onions in 4 tablespoons of butter until soft. Combine ham, crumbs, parsley, thyme, salt, pepper, and eggs with onions and melted butter. Stuff the fish and sew it up. Place fish in a shallow baking pan with enough white wine to completely cover the bottom of pan. Top the fish with strips of salt pork and bake at 350° for 45 minutes, or until fish flakes with fork. While fish is baking, baste occasionally, covering the pan after

16

the first 15 minutes of cooking. When fish is done, remove the salt pork and arrange fish on a platter. Keep warm.

Strain the pan juices into a small saucepan. Thicken over low heat with 2 tablespoons softened butter kneaded into 3 tablespoons of flour. Stir in the lightly beaten egg yolks and continue stirring until well blended. Do not let the sauce boil. Check for seasoning, and add lemon juice and chopped parsley. Pour over the fish. Serve immediately. *Serves 4.*

MENU

❧

Indian Peanut Bass

Green Corn Casserole

*Mixed Green Salad
with Mustard Dressing*

Peanut Butter Bread

Crowned Cherry Tarts

INDIAN PEANUT BASS

2 pounds bass fillets
3 cups Court Bouillon
3 tablespoons peanut oil
3 tablespoons flour
1 teaspoon curry powder
1 cup milk
½ cup cream
2 tablespoons butter
Salt and pepper to taste
4 tablespoons chopped Spanish peanuts

Place the fish fillets in a shallow pan. Cover with 2 cups boiling Court Bouillon. Bring to a boil. Lower heat and simmer 15 minutes. Remove fillets from bouillon and keep warm.

In a saucepan over low heat, blend the peanut oil and flour. Stir in curry powder. Add milk and 1 cup reserved Court Bouillon. When sauce begins to thicken, whisk in cream, butter, and salt and pepper. Place fillets on warm serving platter. Cover with sauce and sprinkle with chopped peanuts. *Serves 6.*

COURT BOUILLON

4 cups water
1 cup white wine
2 pounds fish trimmings
1 clove garlic
4 sprigs parsley
1 small onion
6 peppercorns
½ teaspoon salt
1 bay leaf
½ lemon, sliced

Place all ingredients in a heavy saucepan. Bring to a boil. Lower heat. Cover and simmer for 30 minutes. Remove from heat. Strain, using cheesecloth or a fine sieve. Discard all but the clear broth. Bouillon will keep, tightly covered and refrigerated, for 3 days. May be frozen. *Makes approximately 1 quart.*

GREEN CORN CASSEROLE

3 ears tender young green corn
1 teaspoon sugar
1 teaspoon salt
1 inch of a cinnamon stick
1 cup cream
3 eggs, separated

Preheat oven to 350°. Slice corn from ears. Put corn, sugar, salt, and cinnamon in a saucepan; pour in cream to barely cover. Cook for 15 minutes over low heat. Stir constantly to prevent sticking. Beat egg whites until stiff. Add yolks to beaten whites, one at a time, while still beating. Discard cinnamon from corn. Gently fold corn into eggs. Pour into a well-buttered 6-cup casserole. Set in pan of hot water and bake, at 350°, for about 1 hour, or until golden brown and firm. Serve in casserole. *Serves 6.*

MIXED GREEN SALAD WITH MUSTARD DRESSING

6 cups chopped mixed salad greens
1 recipe Mustard Dressing

Toss greens with dressing and serve immediately. *Serves 6.*

MUSTARD DRESSING

¾ cup olive oil
¼ cup fruit vinegar
3 tablespoons fine French mustard
1 teaspoon fresh lemon juice
1 teaspoon minced fresh shallots

Whisk all ingredients together. Refrigerate, covered, until ready to use. *Enough to cover six cups of greens.*

PEANUT BUTTER BREAD

2 cups flour
4 teaspoons baking powder
1 teaspoon salt
¼ cup sugar
1¼ cups milk
⅔ cup peanut butter

Preheat oven to 350°. Sift flour, baking powder, salt, and sugar together. Add milk to peanut butter and blend well. Add to dry ingredients. Beat thoroughly. The dough must be soft enough to take the shape of the pan. Bake in greased bread loaf pan at 350° for 45 to 50 minutes, or until light brown. Remove from pan and cool on wire rack. Keeps, tightly wrapped and refrigerated, for at least a week. May be frozen. *Makes 1 loaf.*

CROWNED CHERRY TARTS

2 *tablespoons cornstarch*
3 *tablespoons sugar*
1 *cup cherry juice*
1 *tablespoon butter*
2 *cups canned sweet cherries*
1 *recipe Plain Pastry (see page 8)*

Mix cornstarch and sugar together in a medium saucepan. Gradually add juice and cook, over low heat, until smooth and thick. Add butter and cook about 3 minutes to blend. Add cherries. Set aside to cool.

Preheat oven to 450°. Divide dough into 2 parts. Roll one out on a floured board. Cut into 8 rounds large enough to fit either muffin or tart pans. Trim edges and prick thoroughly with fork. Bake at 450° for approximately 15 minutes, or until light brown. Remove from heat. Set aside.

Roll out remaining dough. Using a scallop-edged cutter, cut out enough pastry rounds to fit top of filled tarts. Using a smaller circle cutter, cut out center of scallop. Bake cut-out scallops on a cookie sheet at 450° for approximately 5 minutes or until light brown.

Pour cherry mixture into baked tart shells. Place a baked "crown" on top of each. *Serves 8.*

MENU

❧

Bass
with Mint Honey Sauce

Boiled New Potatoes

Goldenrod Beans

New Orleans Pecan Pie

BASS WITH MINT HONEY SAUCE

4 pounds bass fillets
1 cup whole wheat flour
$1/4$ teaspoon freshly ground black pepper
$1/2$ cup peanut oil
$1/4$ teaspoon ground rosemary
　Juice of 3 lemons
6 tablespoons raisins
1 cup water
2 tablespoons honey
4 tablespoons salted sunflower seeds
1 clove garlic, finely minced
1 tablespoon chopped fresh mint

Pat fillets dry with paper towel. Dredge in flour. Sprinkle with pepper and set aside. Pour oil into heavy skillet. Stir in rosemary and heat, over high heat, until smoking. Fry fish for approximately 2 to 3 minutes, or until golden brown on both sides. Remove from oil and drain on paper towel. Keep warm.

In a heavy saucepan, over medium heat, bring lemon juice, raisins, water, honey, sunflower seeds, and garlic to a boil. Place fried fish in a deep skillet. Pour sauce on the fish and simmer, over low heat, for approximately 5 minutes. Remove from heat and place on serving platter. Sprinkle with mint. *Serves 6.*

GOLDENROD BEANS

1½ pounds whole green beans
1½ tablespoons butter
2 tablespoons flour
½ teaspoon salt
⅛ teaspoon pepper
3 hard-boiled eggs, shelled
¾ cup evaporated milk
¾ cup mayonnaise

Cook beans in boiling salted water until tender. Save ½ cup cooking liquid. Melt butter, and blend in flour, salt, and pepper. Add bean stock and cook until thick, stirring constantly. Chop egg whites and add to sauce. Stir in milk and heat thoroughly. Remove from heat and add mayonnaise. Pour sauce over beans, and sprinkle with sieved egg yolk. *Serves 6.*

NOTE: Cauliflower, asparagus, or broccoli may be used instead of green beans. Sauce may also be flavored with ½ cup grated cheddar cheese and ¼ teaspoon Worcestershire sauce.

NEW ORLEANS PECAN PIE

    4 *eggs, lightly beaten*
    ½ *cup sugar*
    1½ *cups corn syrup*
    ⅓ *cup butter*
    1 *teaspoon vanilla*
    1¼ *teaspoons fresh lemon juice*
    1⅓ *cups pecan halves*
      1 *9-inch unbaked pie shell (see Plain Pastry, page 8)*
        Whipped cream, optional

Preheat oven to 350°. Combine eggs, sugar, corn syrup, butter, vanilla, and lemon juice, and mix well. Fold in pecans. Pour mixture into pie shell. Bake approximately 50 minutes, or until filling is set and top is light brown. Serve with fresh whipped cream. *Serves 6 to 8.*

OTHER RECIPES

CRISPY BACON BASS

1 2- to 2½-pound dressed bass, head on
4 slices bacon
1 small onion, sliced
1 clove garlic, minced
2 cups canned tomatoes, drained
½ teaspoon oregano leaves
¼ teaspoon sugar
  Salt and pepper to taste
1 tablespoon chopped fresh parsley

Preheat oven to 425°. In skillet, over medium heat, fry bacon until crisp. When done, remove bacon from pan, drain on paper towel, and crumble. Set aside. Sauté onion and garlic in bacon fat until tender. Stir in tomatoes, oregano, sugar, salt, pepper, and parsley. Simmer over low heat for 5 minutes, stirring to break up tomatoes. Add bacon. Place bass on sheet of heavy duty aluminum foil large enough to enclose fish. Spoon ½ cup tomato sauce into fish cavity. Spoon remaining sauce over top. Wrap in aluminum foil. Place on baking sheet. Bake 25 to 35 minutes, or until fish flakes easily with fork. Remove from heat and serve immediately. *Serves 2.*

Bass with Crunchy Walnut Sauce

2 pounds largemouth or smallmouth bass fillets, ½ to 1 inch thick,
    skin removed
    Salt and pepper to taste
1 cup sliced fresh mushrooms
½ cup sliced celery
¼ cup finely chopped onion
3 tablespoons butter or margarine
3 tablespoons flour
½ teaspoon salt
½ teaspoon dried basil leaves, or 1 teaspoon chopped fresh basil
½ teaspoon dry mustard
2 cups light cream
½ cup coarsely chopped walnuts
    Celery tops, for garnish

Preheat oven to 350°. Line a 13-by-9-by-2-inch baking pan with heavy duty aluminum foil. Sprinkle fillets with salt and pepper. Place fillets, skinned-side down, in pan. In a skillet, over medium heat, sauté mushrooms, celery, and onion in butter until tender. Stir in flour, salt, basil and mustard. Add cream. Cook until thick, stirring constantly. Pour over fish fillets. Bake at 350° for 25 to 30 minutes, or until fish flakes easily with fork. Sprinkle with walnuts. Place under broiler for 2 minutes, or until walnuts are toasted. Garnish with celery tops if desired. *Serves 4 to 6.*

MENU

❧

Judy Basten's Beer Belly Perch

Zucchini with Sour Cream and Dill

Boxty in the Pan

Raspberry Bavarian Cake

JUDY BASTEN'S BEER BELLY PERCH

 3 *pounds perch fillets*
1¼ *cups self-rising flour*
 1 *tablespoon sugar*
 1 *teaspoon dry mustard*
 ¼ *teaspoon cayenne pepper*
 1 *egg, beaten*
 1 *cup beer*
1½ *cups vegetable oil*
   Salt and pepper to taste

Pat fillets dry with paper towel. Set aside. Mix flour, sugar, mustard, and cayenne pepper together. Beat egg and beer. Slowly pour mixture into dry ingredients, stirring constantly to make a smooth batter. Heat vegetable oil in a heavy skillet over high heat until smoking.

27

Dip fillets, one at a time, into batter. Let excess drip off and immediately place fillets in hot oil. Fry for approximately 2 to 3 minutes, or until golden brown on both sides. Do not crowd pan. Drain on paper towels. Season with salt and pepper. *Serves 6.*

NOTE: If regular flour is used, add 2 teaspoons baking powder and ½ teaspoon salt.

ZUCCHINI WITH SOUR CREAM AND DILL

½ cup butter
6 medium zucchini, thinly sliced
2 tablespoons finely chopped fresh dill
  Salt and pepper to taste
8 ounces sour cream

Melt butter in medium saucepan over low heat. Raise heat to medium and sauté zucchini, sprinkling with dill, salt, and pepper to taste. Cook until fork tender. Stir in sour cream and heat through. Serve immediately. *Serves 6.*

BOXTY IN THE PAN

1 pound raw potatoes
2 cups cooked, mashed potatoes
4 cups flour
  Salt and pepper to taste
¼ cup melted butter or bacon fat

Preheat oven to 300°. Peel the raw potatoes and grate into a clean cloth. Wring them tightly over a bowl, catching all liquid. Put the grated potatoes into another bowl and spread with the cooked, mashed potatoes. When the starch has sunk to the bottom of the raw potato liquid, pour off the water and scrape starch onto the potatoes. Mix well. Sift the flour, salt, and pepper into potatoes. Mix well. Add the melted butter or fat. Knead. Roll out on a floured board and shape into round, flat cakes. Make a deep cross on the top, so that when cooked they will divide easily. Bake on a greased

cookie sheet at 300° for about 40 minutes or until golden brown.
Serve hot with butter. *Serves 6.*

RASPBERRY BAVARIAN CAKE

1½ *tablespoons unflavored gelatin*
¼ *cup cold water*
2 *cups milk*
2 *eggs, separated*
¾ *cup sugar*
1 *teaspoon lemon juice*
1 *cup fresh raspberries*
½ *cup heavy cream, whipped*
½ *cup whipped cream, optional*
¼ *cup fresh raspberries, optional*

Soften gelatin in water for 5 minutes. Scald milk, add gelatin
and stir until dissolved. Mix egg yolks with sugar and gradually add
hot milk. Cook, in the top half of double boiler, over boiling water
for 3 minutes, or until mixture coats a spoon. Remove from heat
and chill.

When mixture begins to thicken, stir in lemon juice and raspberries. Beat egg whites until stiff and fold, with heavy cream, into
raspberry mixture. Pour into buttered springform pan and chill until
firm. Unmold. Garnish, if desired, with whipped cream rosettes and
fresh raspberries. Slice to serve. *Serves 6 to 8.*

NOTE: For Apricot Bavarian Cake use 1 cup cooked apricot purée in place
of raspberries.

OTHER RECIPES

❦

DEVILED PERCH FILLETS

16 perch fillets
½ cup Worcestershire sauce
   Juice of 3 lemons
¼ cup steak sauce
½ cup chili sauce
¼ teaspoon cayenne
 1 teaspoon dry mustard
 1 teaspoon freshly ground black pepper
   Salt to taste
 1 cup buttered bread crumbs
¼ cup softened butter

Preheat oven to 425°. Mix the Worcestershire sauce, lemon juice, steak sauce, chili sauce, cayenne, mustard, and black pepper and spread on the fillets. Let stand for ½ hour.

Place the fillets in a greased baking dish. Bake at 425° for 20 minutes or until fish is flaky. A few minutes before the fish is done, add salt to taste. Remove the pan from the oven, sprinkle with buttered crumbs, dot with butter, and place under broiler to brown. *Serves 8.*

OCEAN PERCH WITH ORANGE SAUCE

 2 pounds ocean perch fillets
 3 tablespoons olive oil
 1 clove garlic, minced
 1 teaspoon lemon juice
   Juice of 1 orange
   Rind of 1 orange, finely minced
½ teaspoon peeled and grated fresh ginger root, or ½ teaspoon
   ground ginger
 1 cup Court Bouillon (see page 19)

30

2 teaspoons cornstarch
2 teaspoons cold water

Preheat broiler. Using 1 tablespoon olive oil, coat the fish fillets on both sides. Place in broiling pan. Broil, 4 inches from heat, for about 3 to 4 minutes on each side or until fish flakes easily, turning once. When done, place on a serving platter and keep warm.

In a heavy skillet, over medium heat, heat the remaining 2 tablespoons of oil. Add the garlic. Lower heat and sauté until garlic is soft but not brown. Add the lemon juice, orange juice, orange rind, ginger, and Court Bouillon. Cook for 5 minutes, stirring frequently. Mix the cornstarch with cold water and add to the sauce. Cook until thick, stirring constantly. Remove from heat and pour over fish. Serve immediately. *Serves 6.*

MENU

❦

Lemon Tarragon King Crappie

Ranger Garlic Grits

Cucumber-Radish Slaw

Raspberry Jam Cake

LEMON TARRAGON KING CRAPPIE

4 whole crappie
2 cups water
½ teaspoon pepper
1 teaspoon salt
1 bay leaf
  Juice of 1 lemon
1 teaspoon chopped fresh tarragon

Combine water, pepper, salt, bay leaf, and half of the lemon juice in a large pot. Bring to a boil and cook for about 3 minutes. Reduce heat. Place fish in a fish-steaming basket or wrap in cheesecloth. Gently place in simmering water. Cover and cook 6 to 10 minutes or until fish is firm but flakes easily. Remove from water. Uncover. Place one fish on each serving plate.

Mix tarragon and remaining lemon juice. Sprinkle equal portions over each fish. Serve immediately. *Serves 4.*

RANGER GARLIC GRITS

3 cups water
¾ teaspoon salt
1 cup quick-cooking grits
1 16-ounce roll garlic cheese
2 eggs
¼ cup butter
¼ cup milk
   Cayenne pepper to taste
¼ cup grated sharp cheddar cheese
   Paprika

Preheat oven to 300°. Grease an 8-by-10-inch baking dish. In a medium saucepan, over high heat, bring water to a boil. Add salt and grits. Stirring constantly, cook for 5 minutes, or until done. Remove from heat and stir in garlic cheese, eggs, butter, milk, and cayenne pepper to taste. Pour into prepared baking dish and bake, at 300°, for 45 minutes. Remove from oven. Sprinkle top with grated sharp cheddar cheese and paprika. Return to oven to melt topping. When melted, remove from heat and serve immediately. *Serves 4 to 6.*

CUCUMBER-RADISH SLAW

3 large cucumbers, peeled, seeded, and grated
1 cup grated white radish
½ cup thinly sliced red radishes
½ cup chopped sweet red pepper
¼ teaspoon celery seed
1 teaspoon olive oil
¾ cup yogurt
   Salt and pepper to taste

Mix all ingredients together to blend. Add salt and pepper to taste. Refrigerate, covered, for one hour before serving. If slaw gets too liquid, drain before serving. *Serves 4 to 6.*

RASPBERRY JAM CAKE

¾ *cup butter*
1½ *cups dark brown sugar*
6 *eggs*
3 *cups sifted all-purpose flour*
1½ *teaspoons baking soda*
½ *teaspoon ground cinnamon*
½ *teaspoon grated nutmeg*
¼ *teaspoon ground cloves*
½ *teaspoon lemon juice*
4 *tablespoons heavy cream*
2 *cups seedless raspberry jam*
1 *cup currants*
1 *tablespoon flour*
1 *recipe Lemon Icing*

Preheat oven to 375°. Beat the butter until light and fluffy. Cream in the sugar. Separate the eggs, reserving the whites. Beat the yolks until lemon colored and add to the butter and sugar. Combine the sifted flour with the baking soda, cinnamon, nutmeg, and cloves; sift again. Set aside. Stir the lemon juice into the cream and place in the oven for a few minutes to let the cream curdle. Remove and blend with 1½ cups seedless jam. Alternately add the dry ingredients and the jam mixture to the creamed butter and sugar mixture, stirring well after each addition. Sprinkle the currants with 1 tablespoon of flour and mix into the batter. Beat the egg whites until stiff but not dry, then gently fold into the batter.

Lightly grease two 8-inch cake pans. Divide the batter between them and bake, at 375°, for about 30 minutes or until the top springs back when lightly pressed. Cool, in the pan, for 15 minutes. Remove from pan and cool further on wire racks. Spread remaining ½ cup raspberry jam between layers before frosting with Lemon Icing. *Serves 8 to 12.*

LEMON ICING

1 *cup butter*
4 *egg yolks*
4 *cups sifted confectioners' sugar*
¼ *cup lemon juice*

Beat the butter until light and fluffy. Beat in the egg yolks. Blend in the sugar and lemon juice. Continue to beat until all the ingredients are well blended and the icing is smooth. Spread on cooled cake. Refrigerate icing if not using immediately. *Makes enough for one 8-inch two-layer cake.*

MENU

❦

Door County Style Fish Boil

Fresh Corn on the Cob

Caraway Slaw

Indian Corn Muffins

Waupaca Blueberry Pie

DOOR COUNTY STYLE FISH BOIL

6 pounds salmon or whitefish, cut into steaks
3 pounds small or medium red potatoes, quartered
2 pounds small Spanish onions
  Salt and pepper to taste

Dig a pit and clear an area about 2-foot square for building an outdoor fire. Using soft wood as a starter, build a roaring fire, then add hard-wood logs to maintain the fire. Place an iron grate over the fire.

Fill a large cast iron pot three-quarters full of water and bring to a boil over fire.

Place potatoes in a wire cooking basket that will fit into the cast iron pot. Lower basket into pot. Cook at a full rolling boil for about 3 to 4 minutes. Remove basket and add onions. Place back in pot. Add a good handful of salt and continue boiling for 3 minutes.

Remove basket and add fish. Again lower into pot and cook for 4 to 5 minutes, or until the fish and potatoes are fork tender. Ask crowd to stand back. Throw 3 ounces of kerosene onto the fire for the final boil-over. This boil-over will eliminate the oils and salt. Serve immediately. *Serves 8 to 10.*

CARAWAY SLAW

4 cups shredded green cabbage
4 cups shredded red cabbage
½ cup minced red onion
1 tablespoon caraway seed
1 teaspoon celery seed
1 teaspoon grated fresh horseradish
½ cup plain yogurt
¼ cup sour cream
½ cup mayonnaise
1 tablespoon fresh lemon juice

Combine the cabbages and onion. Toss in all remaining ingredients. Stir to blend. Refrigerate, covered, until ready to serve. *Serves 10.*

INDIAN CORN MUFFINS

2 cups cornmeal
2 cups sifted all-purpose flour
1 teaspoon salt
1½ teaspoons baking powder
2 cups milk
4 eggs, beaten
¼ cup melted butter

Preheat oven to 400°. Sift dry ingredients into a mixing bowl. Combine milk with eggs and add to the dry ingredients. Add melted butter and stir until blended. Grease and flour 2-inch muffin tins. Pour in batter and bake, at 400°, for 20 minutes, or until light brown. *Makes 24 muffins.*

WAUPACA BLUEBERRY PIE

8 cups blueberries
2 cups sugar
½ cup flour
3 tablespoons lemon juice
2 9-inch unbaked pie shells with lids (see Plain Pastry, page 8)

Preheat oven to 450°. Mix berries with sugar, flour, and lemon juice. Pour berries into pie shells and cover with top crusts. Prick tops with a fork. Bake at 450° for 10 minutes. Reduce oven to 350° and bake 20 to 30 minutes longer or until crusts are light brown and pies are bubbling. *Serves 8 to 12.*

MENU

❧

Citrus River Salmon

Brown Rice

Sugar Snap Peas 'n' Carrots

*Mixed Green Salad with Manion
Vinaigrette*

Winchester Custard Pie

CITRUS RIVER SALMON

2 *pounds salmon fillets, cut into 6 pieces*
½ *cup all-purpose flour*
  Salt and pepper to taste
3 *tablespoons chopped fresh parsley*
¼ *cup olive oil*
1 *tablespoon fresh lime juice*
4 *cloves garlic, crushed*
  Juice of 4 medium oranges

Preheat oven to 450°. Dredge the fillet pieces in flour seasoned with salt and pepper. Mix together parsley, olive oil, lime juice, and garlic. Place fish in a buttered casserole dish. Spread parsley mixture on both sides of fish. Pour on orange juice. Cover and bake at 450° for 20 minutes or until fish begins to flake. Serve immediately over brown rice. *Serves 6.*

39

SUGAR SNAP PEAS 'N' CARROTS

3 cups sugar snap peas
2 cups peeled carrots, sliced diagonally or crinkle edged
½ teaspoon grated fresh lemon peel
½ teaspoon crushed lemon pepper
2 tablespoons melted butter

Separately steam the peas and carrots until just crisp. Mix together with the lemon peel, lemon pepper, and butter. Serve immediately. *Serves 6.*

MIXED GREEN SALAD WITH MANION VINAIGRETTE

6 cups torn mixed greens, such as romaine, escarole, red or green leaf lettuce, spinach, arugula, rocket, chicory, watercress, butter lettuce, dandelion, or any home-grown or wild lettuce or green that can be eaten raw, washed and dried
1 recipe Manion Vinaigrette

Make certain that the greens are well washed and dried before tearing. Mix them together in a salad bowl. Lightly toss greens and Manion Vinaigrette together. Serve immediately. *Serves 6.*

MANION VINAIGRETTE

½ cup fresh olive oil
¼ cup tarragon vinegar
2 tablespoons fresh orange juice
1 teaspoon fresh lemon juice
1 teaspoon Dijon mustard
Salt and pepper to taste

Whisk all ingredients together. Store, covered, in the refrigerator until ready to use. It will keep for up to one week. *Makes approximately 1 cup.*

WINCHESTER CUSTARD PIE

¾ cup butter
½ cup sugar
6 eggs, separated
1 cup wild goose plum preserves
2 tablespoons whiskey
½ cup cream
1 9-inch unbaked pie shell (see Plain Pastry, page 8)
   Whipped cream, optional

Preheat oven to 400°. Cream butter and sugar. Beat egg yolks and add to creamed mixture. Stir in plum preserves, whiskey, and ½ cup cream. Beat egg whites until stiff and fold into mixture. Bake pie crust at 400° for 15 minutes. Remove from oven and fill with custard mixture. Reduce oven temperature to 375° and continue baking 40 minutes or until knife inserted in center comes out clean. Let cool. Spread with whipped cream before serving, if desired. *Serves 6 to 8.*

OTHER RECIPES

SALMON PARTY PILAF

1 pound poached salmon, boned, skinned, and flaked
2 tablespoons butter
1 cup sliced celery
1/3 cup minced onion
1 large green pepper, cut into slivers
1/2 cup sliced fresh mushrooms
3 cups cooked rice
1/3 cup diced canned pimento
1/2 cup sliced Brazil nuts
   Salt and pepper to taste
1/2 teaspoon dried rosemary
1/2 teaspoon dried marjoram

Melt butter in skillet over medium heat. Add celery, onion, green pepper, and mushrooms. Sauté for 3 minutes or until tender-crisp.

Add salmon, rice, pimento, Brazil nuts, salt, pepper, rosemary, and marjoram. Heat to serving temperature. Serve immediately. *Serves 6 to 8.*

SALMON QUICHE

8 ounces cooked salmon (cooked tuna, shrimp, crabmeat, or
   lobster may be used)
1 9-inch unbaked pie shell (see Plain Pastry, page 8)
3 slices bacon, diced
1/2 cup grated cheddar cheese
2 tablespoons chopped scallions
3 eggs
1/2 cup plain yogurt
1 cup light cream and any fish liquid
   Salt and white pepper to taste

⅛ teaspoon ground fennel
Paprika

Preheat oven to 400°. Bake pie shell at 400° for 5 minutes. Remove from oven and allow to cool. Reduce oven temperature to 350°.

Fry bacon until crisp. Drain and set aside. Flake salmon evenly over bottom of pie shell. Cover with bacon, cheese, and scallions.

Beat eggs. Add yogurt, light cream, fish liquid, salt, pepper, and fennel. Pour over the seafood and sprinkle top with paprika. Bake at 350° for 45 minutes or until set. *Serves 6.*

ROSALIE KOTOWICH'S SALMON PORCUPINES

½ pound ground, raw pink salmon
¼ cup uncooked rice
¼ cup grated raw carrot
1½ tablespoons finely chopped onion
1 small egg
  Salt and pepper to taste
5 ounces cream of mushroom soup (soup mix or canned soup)
¼ cup water

Preheat oven to 350°. Blend together the salmon, rice, carrots, onions, and egg. Season to taste. Shape into 4 large fish balls. Place in deep-sided buttered casserole. Leave space between fish balls for the expansion of rice during cooking. Mix soup with water and ladle over. Cover casserole and bake at 350° for 1 hour. *Serves 2 to 3.*

MENU

❦

Chipped Bluegill Cups
Caraway Potato Wafers
Steamed Broccoli Flowers
Old-Fashioned Chocolate Pudding

CHIPPED BLUEGILL CUPS

1½ cups cooked, flaked bluegill
3 tablespoons butter
3 eggs, separated
1 cup heavy cream
1½ cups saltine cracker crumbs
1 teaspoon onion juice
1 teaspoon Worcestershire sauce
1 teaspoon lemon juice
1 pinch nutmeg
Salt to taste
Paprika
1 recipe Mornay Sauce

Preheat oven to 350°. Cream the fish and butter. Add egg yolks, heavy cream, and cracker crumbs. Add the onion juice, Worcestershire sauce, lemon juice, nutmeg, and salt; blend well. Beat egg whites until stiff and fold into the mixture. Pour into a buttered 2-quart mold, allowing room for rising. Sprinkle with paprika. Bake at 350° for 40 minutes or until well risen and slightly brown. Remove from heat. Unmold and place on serving platter. Cover with Mornay Sauce and serve immediately. *Serves 6.*

MORNAY SAUCE

2 *tablespoons butter*
2 *tablespoons flour*
1 *cup milk*
2 *tablespoons heavy cream*
3 *tablespoons grated Gruyère or Parmesan cheese*
  Salt and pepper to taste

In a small saucepan, over medium heat, melt butter. Stir in flour to blend. Lower heat and add the milk, stirring constantly. When sauce begins to thicken, stir in cream, cheese, and salt and pepper to taste. Keep stirring until sauce is thick and creamy. Remove from heat and use immediately. *Makes 1½ cups.*

CARAWAY POTATO WAFERS

1 *cup riced potatoes*
½ *cup butter, softened*
1⅛ *cups flour*
1 *egg, lightly beaten*
1 *tablespoon milk*
  Salt to taste
1 *tablespoon caraway seed*

Preheat oven to 350°. Work potatoes, butter, and flour lightly with fork to make a smooth dough. Set aside ½ hour to chill. Roll out dough ⅛ inch thick. Place on baking sheet. Brush top with egg mixed with milk and sprinkle liberally with salt and caraway seed. Cut with hot knife into narrow strips 1 inch wide and 3 inches long. Place in 350° oven and bake for 5 minutes. Increase heat to 400°. Bake 15 minutes or until crisp and light brown. Remove from heat. Drain on paper towel and serve immediately. *Serves 6.*

OLD-FASHIONED CHOCOLATE PUDDING

2 ounces unsweetened chocolate
1 cup warm milk
½ cup warm heavy cream
1 teaspoon flour
¾ cup sugar
3 egg yolks, beaten
1 teaspoon vanilla
   Whipped cream, optional

Melt the chocolate in top half of double boiler over boiling water. Stir in milk and cream. Combine the flour and sugar. Whisking constantly, blend flour and sugar into chocolate. When smooth, beat ¼ cup chocolate into egg yolks, then add to remaining chocolate. Keep whisking until pudding is smooth and slightly thick. Stir in vanilla. Remove from heat and pour into serving dish. Cover with a sheet of waxed paper and let cool. Serve with whipped cream, if desired. *Serves 6.*

MENU

Broiled Trout Crowns

Batter-Fried Eggplant

Mixed Green Salad
with Manion Vinaigrette (see page 40)

Honey and Nut Bran Muffins

Lemon Mousse

BROILED TROUT CROWNS

6 *brown trout steaks,* 3/4 *inch thick*
1 *teaspoon lemon juice*
  Salt and pepper to taste
2 *egg whites*
3/4 *cup mayonnaise*
3/4 *cup finely grated medium-sharp cheddar cheese*
1/4 *cup chopped green onion*
2 *tablespoons finely chopped parsley*
1 *tablespoon dill weed*
1/4 *teaspoon cayenne pepper*

Preheat broiler. Coat broiling pan liberally with nonstick spray.
Place steaks on pan and sprinkle with lemon juice, salt, and pepper.

Broil, 4 inches from heat, for 3 or 4 minutes on each side, or until fish begins to flake. Remove from heat. Set aside, but keep warm.

Beat egg whites until stiff. Fold in mayonnaise, cheese, green onion, parsley, dill, pinch of salt, and cayenne pepper. Spread mixture evenly on top of each fish steak. Return to broiler and cook until light brown. Remove from heat and serve immediately. *Serves 6.*

BATTER-FRIED EGGPLANT

2 *medium eggplants, peeled*
  Salt
1½ *cups all-purpose flour*
⅛ *teaspoon salt*
3 *eggs*
1 *cup milk*
1 *cup vegetable oil*
1 *lemon, cut into wedges*

Cut eggplant into ¼-inch thick slices. Arrange on a flat surface and sprinkle lightly with salt. Let stand 15 minutes.

Sift flour into a bowl. Add salt. Beat eggs into the flour mixture. Add milk, stirring to thoroughly moisten the batter.

Dry the eggplant slices between paper towels. Dip into the batter. Heat oil in heavy skillet over high heat. Fry eggplant until golden on both sides, turning once. Drain on paper towels. Serve hot with lemon wedges. *Serves 6.*

NOTE: Almost any vegetable can be transformed into a tempting and mouth-watering specialty when prepared this way.

HONEY AND NUT BRAN MUFFINS

1 *cup flour*
¼ *to ½ teaspoon baking soda*
½ *teaspoon salt*
2 *cups bran*
½ *cup honey*
1 *tablespoon melted butter*

1½ cups milk
¾ cup finely chopped walnuts

Preheat oven to 425°. Sift together flour, soda, and salt. Mix with the bran. Stir in remaining ingredients. Blend well. Place in greased large muffin pans and bake at 425° for 25 to 30 minutes or until brown. *Makes 12 muffins.*

LEMON MOUSSE

1 packet unflavored gelatin
¼ cup water
1 cup heavy cream
4 eggs, separated
⅔ cup sugar
⅓ cup fresh lemon juice
1 tablespoon grated fresh lemon rind
  Lemon slices, whipped cream, or fresh mint leaves for garnish,
  optional

Soften gelatin in ¼ cup of water. Whip cream and set aside. Beat egg whites until stiff. Set aside. Beat egg yolks and sugar together until light and frothy. Add gelatin, lemon juice, and rind. Blend well.

Fold whipped cream and beaten egg whites into the mousse. Serve immediately or refrigerate, covered, until ready to serve. Garnish with a lemon slice, a dollop of whipped cream, or fresh mint leaves, if desired. *Serves 6.*

MENU
❧

Stuffed Fish Fillets

Fried Corn
with Sour Cream Sauce

Apple and Nut Salad

Lemon Pound Cake

STUFFED FISH FILLETS

2 *pounds fish fillets*
1 *recipe Herb Stuffing*
1 *cup white wine*
1 *tablespoon cider vinegar*
1 *tablespoon sugar*
  Butter
12 *large shrimp, steamed and peeled*
1 *lemon, cut into wedges*

Split fillets lengthwise, rinse and dry. Prepare stuffing. Spread stuffing on fillets. Roll up jelly-roll style and secure with round wooden toothpicks. Arrange in a large skillet. Combine wine, vinegar, and sugar; pour around the fish. Cover and poach for 15 minutes or until fish is just tender. Carefully remove the fish to a heated serving platter. Garnish with shrimp and lemon and serve immediately. *Serves 4 to 6.*

HERB STUFFING

  4 *tablespoons butter, melted*
  ¾ *cup fresh white bread crumbs*
  1 *cup chopped fresh spinach*
  ¼ *cup chopped fresh parsley*
  1 *tablespoon chopped fresh green herbs of your choice*
  ½ *teaspoon ground mace*
  ¼ *teaspoon ground nutmeg*
  2 *hard-boiled egg yolks, chopped*
  ½ *cup currants*

Combine all ingredients in a bowl and toss gently with a fork until well blended. Use immediately. *Serves 4 to 6.*

FRIED CORN WITH SOUR CREAM SAUCE

  3 *cups cooked whole kernel corn*
  4 *tablespoons butter*
  ⅓ *cup chopped red and green peppers*
  1 *teaspoon chopped onion*
  4 *teaspoons flour*
  1 *cup thick sour cream*
    Salt and pepper to taste

Fry corn in 2 tablespoons butter until crisp. Remove from heat and set aside. Melt remaining butter. Add peppers and onion and cook over low heat, stirring frequently, until tender. Add flour and mix well. Add sour cream and cook over low heat, stirring constantly, until thick. Season with salt and pepper and serve over corn. *Serves 6.*

APPLE AND NUT SALAD

    4 apples, cored and diced
    2 tablespoons lemon juice
    ¾ cup salted almonds
    ¾ cup Pineapple Cream Dressing
    18 large spinach leaves, washed and trimmed

Combine apples, lemon juice, nuts, and dressing. Arrange on a bed of spinach leaves. Serve immediately. *Serves 6.*

PINEAPPLE CREAM DRESSING

    3 egg yolks
    ½ cup sugar
    5 tablespoons lemon juice
    ½ cup unsweetened pineapple juice
    ½ cup heavy cream, whipped

Beat egg yolks and sugar together. Add fruit juices and cook in top half of double boiler over boiling water, until thick. Cool and fold in whipped cream. Refrigerate until ready to use. *Makes 1½ cups.*

LEMON POUND CAKE

    2 cups sweet butter
    1½ cups sugar
    2 eggs
    ⅓ cup cream
    2 cups cake flour
    ½ teaspoon cream of tartar
    2 tablespoons fresh lemon juice
    1 tablespoon grated fresh lemon rind
    Powdered sugar

Preheat oven to 300°. Cream butter and sugar. Add eggs and beat until light and fluffy. Beat in cream. Mix flour and cream of tartar and gradually add to cream mixture. Stir in lemon juice and rind.

Pour into greased and floured tube cake pan. Bake at 300° for about 1 hour and 15 minutes or until light brown. Remove from heat. Unmold and cool on wire rack. Sprinkle top with powdered sugar. *Makes 1 cake.*

OTHER RECIPES

❦

WHITEFISH WITH PIQUANT SAUCE

1 pound whitefish fillets
1 tablespoon vegetable oil
1 tablespoon cider vinegar
2 tablespoons minced onion
   Salt to taste
2 teaspoons Worcestershire sauce
⅓ cup catsup
¼ cup water
1 tablespoon capers
1 cup cooked green peas

Wipe fish with damp cloth or paper towel. Cut into serving pieces. Set aside. Bring oil, vinegar, onion, salt, Worcestershire, catsup, and water to a boil in top part of double boiler over hot water. Add capers and fish. Cover and cook over boiling water about 25 minutes, or until fish is done, stirring gently several times. Add peas and heat thoroughly. Remove from heat. Serve immediately. *Serves 4.*

PIER I FISH CAKES

1½ pounds boneless whitefish
½ cup raw fat pork
1 cup water chestnuts and/or bamboo shoots
1 tablespoon fresh ginger, optional
2 tablespoons slivered almonds
2 tablespoons soy sauce
2 tablespoons cornstarch
1 tablespoon sesame oil
1 cup vegetable oil
1 recipe Sesame Mayonnaise

Grind fish very fine. Grind the pork, which should be rather fat. Chop the water chestnuts or bamboo shoots, ginger, and almonds. Mix together. Add soy sauce, cornstarch, and sesame oil. Form into small cakes. Heat oil to smoking in heavy skillet. Fry cakes in hot fat until golden on both sides. Remove from heat. Drain on paper towels and serve immediately with Sesame Mayonnaise. *Serves 6.*

SESAME MAYONNAISE

1 *cup Homemade Mayonnaise (see page 94)*
1 *teaspoon sesame oil*
¼ *cup chopped scallions*
1 *teaspoon grated fresh ginger*
1 *tablespoon toasted sesame seeds*
½ *teaspoon curry powder*

Whisk all ingredients together. Cover and refrigerate until ready to serve. *Makes approximately 1¼ cups.*

MENU

Garlic-Roasted Red Snapper

Mo Po Patties

Heaven's Gate Salad

Sliced Oranges in Kirsch

GARLIC-ROASTED RED SNAPPER

6 *1½-pound red snappers, cleaned, trimmed, and scaled, with heads on*
12 *small cloves garlic, peeled*
¼ *cup olive oil*
   Salt and pepper to taste
1½ *teaspoons chopped fresh thyme*
2 *cups chopped fresh fennel*
2 *cups Court Bouillon (see page 19), or fresh chicken broth*
½ *cup Pernod*
¼ *cup cognac*
   Parsley, for garnish

Preheat oven to 475°. Insert garlic into fish. Brush inside and outside of fish with olive oil. Sprinkle with salt and pepper. Sprinkle outside of fish with thyme. Fill fish cavities with fennel. Place fish on an oiled rack in a roasting pan. Mix together bouillon, Pernod, and cognac and pour into pan under fish. Cover tightly with aluminum foil. Bake at 475° for 15 minutes. Remove foil and bake 10 minutes longer. Serve fish with pan juices and garnish with parsley, if desired. *Serves 6.*

Mo Po Patties

6 potatoes
2 tablespoons flour
2 tablespoons butter
1 tablespoon grated Swiss cheese
½ teaspoon salt
1 recipe Tomato Sauce

Preheat oven to 400°. Boil potatoes in their jackets. When done, peel and mash. Add flour, butter, grated cheese, and salt. Mix well and shape into thick, round patties. Make a hole in the middle of each. Place patties in a greased, shallow baking dish. Bake at 400° for about 15 minutes or until brown on both sides. Serve with fresh Tomato Sauce poured into the hole. *Serves 6.*

TOMATO SAUCE

2 tablespoons minced onion
½ clove garlic, minced
1 tablespoon olive oil
3 cups peeled, seeded, and chopped fresh tomatoes
Salt and pepper to taste

Sauté onion and garlic in oil for 5 minutes in a heavy skillet over medium heat. Add tomatoes. Lower heat and simmer about 30 minutes or until thick. Stir occasionally. Press through a sieve. Season with salt and pepper and reheat to serve. *Makes about 2 cups.*

HEAVEN'S GATE SALAD

2 tablespoons unflavored gelatin
½ cup cold water
1 tablespoon lemon juice
4 cups peeled, seeded, and chopped fresh tomatoes
1 tablespoon minced onion
  Dash of celery seed
2 cloves
½ teaspoon salt
1 teaspoon sugar
1 head chicory, separated, trimmed, washed, and dried
1 recipe French Dressing
3 ounces cream cheese

Soften gelatin in cold water. Dissolve softened gelatin over hot water. Add lemon juice and cool. Cook tomatoes, onion, celery seed, cloves, salt, and sugar together for 15 minutes over medium heat. Strain through a sieve into gelatin. Stir to blend. Pour into six heart-shaped molds and chill until firm. Toss chicory with French Dressing and arrange on salad plates. Place jellied tomato heart on each plate. With a pastry bag and tube, pipe frilly border of softened cream cheese around edge. *Serves 6.*

FRENCH DRESSING

1 cup olive or salad oil
¼ cup vinegar
½ teaspoon salt
  Cayenne pepper, to taste
¼ teaspoon white pepper
2 tablespoons chopped parsley

Whisk all ingredients together. Refrigerate until ready to use. *Makes 1½ cups.*

SLICED ORANGES IN KIRSCH

6 large navel oranges, peeled and sliced
¼ cup Kirsch (or Cointreau)
1 tablespoon chopped fresh mint leaves
  Powdered sugar
  Whole mint leaves, for garnish

Place sliced oranges in glass bowl with Kirsch and chopped mint. Refrigerate, covered, for about 3 hours. Serve cold, sprinkled with powdered sugar and garnished with fresh mint leaves. *Serves 6.*

OTHER RECIPES

❧

NORTHWOODS CHICKEN-FRIED RED SNAPPER

4 large red snapper fillets
¼ cup vegetable shortening
½ cup flour
1 large onion, sliced
1 clove garlic, minced
3 tablespoons water
  Salt and pepper to taste
1 recipe Gravy

Red snapper is known as mock chicken by those "in the know." In a heavy skillet, heat shortening to smoking over high heat. Cut fillets into serving pieces and dredge in flour. Lower heat and brown fillets in hot grease. Place onion, garlic, and 3 tablespoons water in a Dutch oven. Add the browned fish and salt and pepper. Pour gravy over fish and cover tightly. Simmer over low heat for about 20 minutes or until the fish flakes easily when tested with a fork. Lift fish carefully to a warmed platter and serve immediately. *Serves 4.*

GRAVY

½ cup flour
3 tablespoons vegetable shortening
  Water
  Pinch of ground nutmeg
  Salt and pepper to taste

In a hot, dry frying pan, brown flour. Reduce heat. Add shortening and mix to a paste. Stirring constantly, gradually add enough water to make a thin brown gravy. Add nutmeg, salt, and pepper. Serve immediately. *Serves 4.*

BAKED STUFFED RED SNAPPER

1 4-pound red snapper, cleaned
  Salt and pepper to taste
3 tablespoons softened butter
1 large onion, chopped
1 clove garlic, minced
4 cups dry bread crumbs
1 cup minced cucumber
½ cup chopped toasted almonds
1 teaspoon thyme
  White wine or sherry, optional

Preheat oven to 350°. Rub the inside of fish with salt, pepper, and 1 tablespoon butter. In a heavy skillet, over medium heat, sauté chopped onion and minced garlic in remaining butter until soft. Add onion and garlic to the bread crumbs, cucumber, and almonds. Season with thyme and additional salt and pepper, if desired. Moisten with water or white wine or sherry. Stuff the fish lightly and sew up.

Place in a well-greased baking pan. Add a little white wine or sherry to the pan, if desired. Bake at 350° for 40 minutes or until the fish flakes easily when tested. Baste occasionally with the pan juices, adding more wine or water, and butter if necessary. *Serves 4.*

BAKED RED FISH CREOLE

1 4- to 5-pound red fish
4 slices bacon
3 tablespoons butter
2 large onions, finely chopped
1 clove garlic, minced
3 cups cooked or canned tomatoes
1 bay leaf
2 cloves
½ teaspoon ground thyme
  Salt and pepper to taste
2 hard-boiled eggs, sliced
2 tablespoons sliced black olives

61

Preheat oven to 425°. In a heavy skillet, over medium heat, fry bacon until crisp. Drain on paper towel. Wipe out pan. Add butter. When melted, sauté onions and garlic over medium heat until tender. Rub the tomatoes through a sieve or put them through a food mill and strain to remove seeds. Add to the onions and garlic. Add the bay leaf, cloves, thyme, and salt and pepper to taste. Simmer 30 minutes. Set aside.

Salt and pepper the interior of the fish. Place it in an oiled baking pan. Pour sauce over fish and bake at 425° for 25 minutes or until the fish flakes easily when tested. Baste often during cooking.

Remove the fish to a hot serving platter and garnish with the bacon slices, sliced eggs, and black olives. Pour the sauce around it. If the sauce seems too thick, dilute with a little red wine or water. *Serves 4.*

MENU

❦

Mason-Dixon Catfish

Long-Grain Brown Rice

Bean Chop

Batter-Fried Eggplant (see page 48)

Green Grape Pie

MASON-DIXON CATFISH

4 *whole catfish (10 to 12 ounces each)*
  Salt and pepper to taste
⅓ *cup flour*
¼ *cup vegetable oil*
¼ *cup prepared mustard*
1 *cup apple juice*
2 *bananas, cut into 1½- to 2-inch chunks*
¼ *cup coarsely chopped salted peanuts*
  Chopped parsley

Preheat oven to 350°. Season fish inside and out with salt and pepper. Set aside 1 tablespoon flour and roll fish in remaining flour. Heat oil in large frying pan until hot. Place fish in pan and fry 8 to 10 minutes or until lightly browned. Turn carefully and fry 8 to 10

63

minutes more, or until fish flakes easily. Remove from heat. Drain on paper towels and keep warm.

Blend reserved 1 tablespoon flour and mustard into remaining fat in pan. Stir in apple juice and cook, stirring constantly, about 1 minute or until thick and smooth; add bananas. Place fish in heat-proof serving dish. Spoon sauce over fish and bake at 350° for 5 minutes. Remove from heat and sprinkle with chopped peanuts and parsley. Serve immediately with long-grain brown rice. *Serves 4.*

BEAN CHOP

  1 *pound fresh green beans*
 ½ *pound fresh wax beans*
  2 *teaspoons bacon fat (or use cooking oil)*
 ½ *cup chopped scallions*
  1 *tablespoon minced fresh chives*
 ½ *teaspoon cracked lemon pepper*
 ½ *cup cooked, chopped bacon, smoked ham, or prosciutto*

Blanch beans in a large pot of boiling, salted water for about 3 to 4 minutes, or until crisp tender. Drain immediately and place under cold running water to stop cooking process. Dry on paper towels.

In a food processor, using the steel blade, coarsely chop beans using on/off motion. Do not over chop.

Melt 2 teaspoons of bacon fat in a heavy skillet over medium heat. Add chopped beans and all remaining ingredients. Stir to heat thoroughly. Serve immediately. *Serves 4.*

GREEN GRAPE PIE

1 9-inch unbaked pie shell (see Plain Pastry, page 8)
2 cups wild green grapes, pea size, stemmed, washed, and drained
(Seeds are soft and need not be removed.)
2 cups sugar
1 teaspoon flour
1 small can evaporated milk, undiluted

Preheat oven to 325°. Place grapes in pie shell. Combine sugar and flour. Sprinkle over grapes. Pour milk over flour and sugar. Bake 1 hour at 325° or until pie is set. *Serves 4 to 6.*

MENU

❧

Turtle Bean Soup

Gourmet Fried Oysters

Sliced Tomatoes and Red Onion

Spoehr's Marsh Potato Doughnuts

TURTLE BEAN SOUP

  1 *12-ounce package black turtle beans*
10 *cups cold water*
  1 *cup chopped celery*
  2 *cups chopped onion*
¼ *cup melted butter*
  4 *teaspoons all-purpose flour*
¼ *cup chopped parsley*
  2 *smoked ham hocks*
  2 *medium leeks, thinly sliced (about ¾ cup)*
  2 *bay leaves*
1½ *teaspoons salt*
¼ *teaspoon pepper*
½ *cup dry Madeira or sherry*
10 *lemon slices, optional*
  3 *chopped eggs, optional*

66

Wash and pick through beans. Cover with boiling water and soak overnight. Drain. Place in a large soup pot and add 10 cups cold water. Cover, bring to a boil and cook over low heat for 1½ hours. In a skillet, slowly sauté celery and onion in butter. Blend in flour and parsley. Stir in 2 cups beans with liquid. Add to beans in pot. Stir to mix. Add ham hocks, leeks, bay leaves, salt, and pepper. Cover and simmer 2½ hours, or until beans are cooked. Discard hocks and bay leaves. Drain beans, reserving broth, and put through a sieve or food mill. Return to broth. Stir in Madeira or sherry and heat. Float a lemon slice and sprinkle chopped hard-boiled egg on each serving, if desired. May be served hot or cold. *Serves 8 to 10.*

GOURMET FRIED OYSTERS

40 large oysters, shucked
1 teaspoon minced fresh oregano (or ½ teaspoon dried)
Salt and pepper to taste
2 cups red wine
3 garlic cloves, chopped
½ cup olive oil
2 cups bread crumbs
½ teaspoon garlic powder
¼ teaspoon fresh ground pepper
4 tablespoons melted butter

Place oysters in a glass bowl with oregano, salt, pepper, red wine, and chopped garlic and oil. Cover and marinate for 4 hours. Drain and roll in bread crumbs seasoned with garlic powder and pepper. In a large skillet over low heat, fry oysters in melted butter until golden brown. *Serves 8.*

SLICED TOMATOES AND RED ONION

4 large beefsteak tomatoes, peeled and sliced
2 large sweet red onions, peeled and sliced
3 tablespoons Balsamic vinegar
1 tablespoon chopped fresh basil
Salt and pepper to taste

Mix all ingredients together. Cover and let set for about 1 hour. Serve at room temperature. *Serves 8.*

SPOEHR'S MARSH POTATO DOUGHNUTS

4 *tablespoons butter*
1 *cup hot mashed potatoes*
3 *eggs*
1¼ *cups sugar*
1 *cup milk*
4 *cups flour*
6 *teaspoons baking powder*
1 *teaspoon salt*
½ *teaspoon vanilla*
¼ *teaspoon ground nutmeg*
   Vegetable oil

Add butter to potatoes and beat well. Beat eggs with sugar and stir into potatoes. Add remaining ingredients except vegetable oil. Mix well. Let stand in a cold place for 1 hour.

In a deep fryer, heat about 4 inches of vegetable oil until very hot. On a lightly floured board, roll out dough to about ¼ inch thick. (The dough may take a little more flour.) Cut out with doughnut cutter and drop into hot oil. Cook until golden brown. Drain on paper towels. Serve warm. *Makes approximately 18 dumplings.*

MENU

🦐

Baby Shrimp Sautéed
with Herbs and Vegetables

Butter Lettuce Salad
with Manion Vinaigrette (see page 40)

Southern Lemon Pie

BABY SHRIMP SAUTÉED WITH HERBS AND VEGETABLES

4 cups baby shrimp, peeled and deveined
1/4 cup each julienne strips of leek, carrot, celery, and fennel
1/4 cup plus 3 tablespoons butter
1/2 cup dry white wine
1 teaspoon each finely chopped fresh tarragon or basil leaves (or
    1/2 teaspoon each, dried)
1 teaspoon finely chopped fresh parsley
1 large garlic clove, crushed
1/4 teaspoon salt
1/8 teaspoon pepper
1 teaspoon finely chopped fresh sorrel or spinach
1 teaspoon all-purpose flour
1 tablespoon softened butter
6 baked puff pastry shells
    Chopped parsley, for garnish

69

Pat shrimp dry with paper towel. Set aside. Stir-fry the julienne vegetables in a wok or frying pan in 3 tablespoons butter for 1 minute. Add wine and simmer for 3 minutes. Remove from heat and keep warm. Melt ¼ cup butter in a skillet over medium heat. Add shrimp and sauté until almost done, about 3 minutes. Add herbs, seasonings and vegetables. Blend flour and softened butter together. Push shrimp and vegetables to the side of the skillet and whisk in butter and flour. Stir until slightly thick. Spoon into puff pastry shells and sprinkle with parsley, if desired. Serve immediately. *Serves 6.*

SOUTHERN LEMON PIE

½ cup sugar
⅓ cup flour
1¼ cups boiling water
1 tablespoon butter
3 egg yolks
1 lemon, juice and grated rind
1 9-inch baked pie shell (see Plain Pastry, page 8)
1 recipe Meringue II

Preheat oven to 425°. Mix sugar and flour in top of double boiler over boiling water. Gradually add boiling water, stirring constantly. Whisk in butter. Beat egg yolks slightly and add to mixture. Cook until thick. Remove from heat and cool. Add lemon juice and rind. Pour into shell, top with meringue and bake at 425°, for 15 minutes or until meringue is golden. *Serves 4 to 6.*

MERINGUE II

3 egg whites
6 tablespoons sugar
½ teaspoon vanilla or other flavoring

Beat egg whites until frothy. Add sugar gradually and continue beating until stiff. Add flavoring. Cover top of pie. Bake immediately. *Serves 4 to 6.*

MENU

❧

Alaskan Crab Cakes

Countryside Creamed Potatoes

Colorado Fried Corn

Frozen Fruit

ALASKAN CRAB CAKES

2 *cups cooked crabmeat*
1 *egg*
½ *cup finely crushed saltine crackers*
⅓ *cup milk*
½ *teaspoon dry mustard*
⅛ *teaspoon white pepper*
⅛ *teaspoon cayenne pepper*
1 *tablespoon Worcestershire sauce*
2 *tablespoons finely chopped parsley*
4 *tablespoons butter*
  Lemon wedges, for garnish

Blend egg, crushed crackers, milk, dry mustard, white pepper, cayenne, and Worcestershire sauce. Stir in crabmeat and parsley. Shape into small patties and lay on a plate covered with waxed paper. Chill for 30 minutes. In a large skillet, melt butter over medium heat. Fry cakes for about 6 to 8 minutes, or until golden brown on both sides. Drain on paper towel and serve hot, garnished with lemon wedges. *Serves 4.*

COUNTRYSIDE CREAMED POTATOES

2 tablespoons butter
¾ cup heavy cream
¾ cup milk
5 medium potatoes, peeled and thinly sliced
½ teaspoon salt
⅛ teaspoon black pepper

Melt butter in a medium-size heavy skillet, taking care not to brown it. Add cream and milk. Heat, over the lowest possible flame; do not boil. Slip the potato slices into the hot cream one at a time until evenly distributed. The liquid should barely cover the potatoes. Season with half the salt and pepper. Simmer for 30 minutes.

Turn the potatoes carefully. Season with remaining salt and pepper, and simmer for 30 minutes more. *Serves 4.*

COLORADO FRIED CORN

3 cups cut, cooked corn
  Salt and pepper to taste
3 tablespoons green pepper
4 tablespoons olive oil

Combine corn, salt, pepper, and green pepper. Sauté in olive oil for 20 minutes, stirring occasionally. *Serves 4.*

FROZEN FRUIT

½ cup sliced strawberries (or whole raspberries)
½ cup diced pineapple
½ cup diced orange segments

½ *cup diced bananas*
2 *teaspoons lemon juice*
1 *packet unflavored gelatin*
1 *tablespoon cold water*
4 *teaspoons strained honey*
⅔ *cup heavy cream, whipped*

Combine fruits and lemon juice and chill. Soften gelatin in cold water. Place in cup and set in a small container of hot water until dissolved. Add to honey. Gently stir gelatin and honey into fruit. Fold in whipped cream and pour into freezer tray. Freeze, covered, for 3 hours or until firm. When ready to serve, unmold and cut into serving portions. Top with additional whipped cream and a slice of fresh fruit, if desired. *Serves 4 to 6.*

OTHER RECIPES

✿

Sweet and Sour Carp

1 4- to 5-pound carp, cleaned
⅔ cup olive oil
4 shallots, chopped
2 large onions, chopped
4 tablespoons flour
2 cups white wine
2 cups water
1 teaspoon salt
    Cayenne pepper
    Grated nutmeg
1 bay leaf
    Pinch of thyme
2 cloves garlic, crushed
¾ cup olive oil
2 tablespoons chopped fresh parsley
½ cup seedless raisins
½ cup currants or sultana raisins
⅓ cup wine vinegar
2 tablespoons brown sugar

This is one of the oldest recipes for carp.

Cut the carp into 2-inch slices. Heat ⅔ cup of olive oil in a large skillet or deep Dutch oven over medium heat. Add the shallots and onions and sauté until soft. Add the flour and blend thoroughly. Gradually stir in the wine and water, and continue cooking, stirring constantly, until thick. Add salt, cayenne, and nutmeg. Bring to a boil. Add the pieces of fish, bay leaf, thyme, and crushed garlic. Simmer for 20 minutes. Remove the carp and arrange it on a long, deep serving dish. Discard bay leaf.

Reduce the sauce, over medium heat, to one-third. With a whisk or electric mixer at medium speed, beat in ¾ cup of olive oil as if you were making mayonnaise. When thoroughly blended, add the parsley, raisins, currants, wine vinegar, and brown sugar. Pour over the carp. Cover and refrigerate. Serve cold. *Serves 4 to 6.*

FISH BALLS WITH HERB SAUCE

4 ounces flaked cooked cod
1 egg, beaten
12 saltines, crushed into crumbs
2 tablespoons water
1 teaspoon lemon juice
1 teaspoon chopped fresh parsley
¼ teaspoon sweet Hungarian paprika
  Dash of pepper
1 recipe Herb Sauce

Preheat oven to 350°. In bowl combine all ingredients. Spray a 9-inch pie pan or shallow casserole with nonstick cooking spray. Shape fish mixture into 16 balls. Arrange in the pie pan, cover with foil, and bake 30 minutes at 350°. Remove from oven. Cover with Herb Sauce and serve immediately. *Serves 2.*

HERB SAUCE

1 tablespoon butter or margarine
1 tablespoon flour
1 cup skim milk
1 egg, hard-boiled and chopped
  Salt to taste
½ teaspoon chopped fresh parsley
¼ teaspoon dried dill, or ½ teaspoon chopped fresh dill
  Dash white pepper

Melt butter or margarine in small saucepan over medium heat. Remove pan from heat and stir in flour. Cook 2 minutes over low heat, stirring occasionally. Gradually add milk, stirring briskly with a wire whisk until margarine, flour, and milk are blended. Continue cooking, stirring constantly with a wooden spoon, until sauce thickens. Add chopped egg, salt, parsley, dill, and pepper. Stir to combine. Serve immediately. *Makes approximately 1 cup.*

COD IN MUSTARD SAUCE

2 pounds fresh cod fillets
1 cup White Sauce
1 teaspoon prepared mustard
2 hard-boiled eggs, chopped
  Coarsely ground black pepper
  Chopped fresh dill

Cut fish into 6 portions and drain on paper towels. Prepare White Sauce in a 10-inch skillet and season with mustard. Arrange fish, skin side down, in sauce in skillet. Bring to a boil, reduce heat, cover, and simmer 12 minutes, or until fish is opaque and flakes easily with fork. Spoon some of the sauce on each steak and garnish with eggs, pepper, and dill. Good with mashed, baked, or riced potatoes. *Serves 6.*

WHITE SAUCE

2 tablespoons butter
2 tablespoons flour
1 cup milk or light cream
  Salt and pepper to taste

In a saucepan, over medium heat, melt the butter. Blend in flour. Gradually add milk, whisking constantly, until sauce is thick and smooth. Add salt and pepper to taste. Use immediately. *Serves 6.*

FISH 'N' CHEESE IN A POCKET

½ cup cooked, boned and flaked flounder
2 pita breads, 1 ounce each
¼ cup mild cheddar cheese, broken into pea-size pieces
1 teaspoon lemon juice
1 teaspoon chopped fresh parsley
¼ teaspoon salt

Cut each pita bread one-third of the way around edge to create pocket. Set aside. Combine all remaining ingredients in a bowl and toss well. Fill each pita with half of fish mixture. *Serves 2.*

CRACKED WHEAT STUFFED STRIPER

  1 *4-pound or 2 2-pound whole flounder, filleted*
  ⅔ *cup sliced celery*
  ⅔ *cup grated carrot*
  ¼ *cup chopped onion*
  1 *teaspoon grated orange peel*
  ¼ *cup butter or margarine*
  4 *cups toasted cracked wheat bread cubes*
  ¼ *cup chopped fresh parsley*
  2 *to 3 tablespoons orange juice*
  2 *tablespoons butter or margarine, melted*
    Paprika

Preheat oven to 375°. In a heavy skillet over medium heat, sauté celery, carrot, onion, and orange peel in butter until tender. Stir in bread cubes, parsley, and enough orange juice to moisten. Line a 12-by-9-by-2-inch baking pan with heavy duty aluminum foil. For large fish, place 1 fillet, dark-skin side down, in pan. Top with half of stuffing. Cut a slit lengthwise through center of remaining fillet, leaving 2 inches uncut at each end. Place skin-side up on top of stuffing. For small fish, divide stuffing. Repeat procedure. Spoon remaining stuffing around fish. Brush with butter and sprinkle with paprika. Bake at 375° for 20 to 25 minutes or until fish flakes easily. Remove from heat and serve immediately. *Serves 4.*

FLOUNDER WITH KIWI SAUCE

  2 *skinless flounder fillets*
    Salt and pepper to taste
  ¾ *cup dry white wine, or ¾ cup water with 1 tablespoon lemon juice*
  1 *recipe Kiwi Sauce*
  2 *slices lemon*

Season fillets with salt and pepper. Roll and secure with tooth-picks. Pour wine or water-lemon mixture into saucepan. Place fillets in saucepan and bring to a boil over medium heat. Reduce heat to low, cover and simmer 5 to 8 minutes or until fork pierces flesh of fish easily.

Remove from liquid with slotted spoon. Place on serving platter or individual plates. Serve warm topped with Kiwi Sauce and gar-nished with lemon slices. May be served cold, also. *Serves 2.*

KIWI SAUCE

> 2 *ripe kiwi fruit, peeled and sliced*
> 2 *teaspoons lemon juice*
> 2 *teaspoons vegetable oil*
> ½ *teaspoon Dijon-style mustard*

Combine all ingredients in blender. Mix until smooth. Serve over poached fish or chicken. *Makes approximately ½ cup.*

HALIBUT DELMONICO

> 6 *halibut fillets*
> 1 *onion, sliced*
> 2 *cups milk*
> 2 *tablespoons butter or margarine*
> 2 *tablespoons flour*
> 2 *tablespoons sherry*
> 1 *cup fresh seedless white grapes*
> ½ *cup grated cheddar cheese*
> ½ *cup bread crumbs*
> ¼ *cup butter or margarine*

Preheat oven to 350°. Place the fish fillets in a large kettle with the sliced onion and just enough milk to cover, about 2 cups. Simmer about 8 minutes or until fish is tender but not broken. Grease a large, flat casserole and place the cooked fish in it, reserving the milk.

In a small saucepan, over medium heat, mix butter and flour until bubbly and well blended. Gradually add the reserved milk to

78

make a cream sauce. Blend in sherry and seedless grapes. Pour over fish. Sprinkle generously with grated cheese and bread crumbs and dot with butter. Bake, at 350°, for about 15 minutes or until well heated and crumbs are browned. *Serves 6.*

BROCCOLI FISH CASSEROLE

2 *cups cooked, flaked sea trout*
1½ *cups chopped cooked broccoli*
2 *cups sliced fresh mushrooms*
¼ *cup sliced green onion*
¼ *cup chopped green pepper*
3 *tablespoons melted butter*
1 *cup grated Swiss cheese*
1 *cup light cream*
2 *eggs, beaten*
1½ *teaspoons Worcestershire sauce*
½ *teaspoon dry mustard*
¾ *teaspoon seasoned salt*
⅓ *cup fine dry bread crumbs*

Preheat oven to 350°. Line an 8-by-8-by-2-inch baking pan with lightly greased heavy duty aluminum foil. Layer broccoli in pan. Sauté mushrooms, onion, and green pepper in 1 tablespoon butter until tender. Combine with flaked fish and ½ cup cheese. Spread evenly over broccoli. Whisk cream, eggs, Worcestershire sauce, mustard, and salt together. Pour over fish mixture. Combine remaining butter, cheese, and bread crumbs. Sprinkle over casserole. Bake at 350° for 40 to 45 minutes or until knife inserted in center comes out clean. Remove from heat and serve immediately. *Serves 4 to 6.*

SHARK HUNTER STEAKS WITH LIME PARSLEY

4 shark steaks
2 tablespoons tamari or other aged soy sauce
½ teaspoon ground cumin
1 cup minced fresh parsley
½ cup lime juice
1 cup olive oil
1 2-inch piece fresh ginger, cut into ⅛-inch-thick slices
1⅓ cups sour cream
1 lime, thinly sliced, optional

Preheat broiler. Set broiler rack as close as possible to heating element. Combine tamari, cumin, parsley, lime juice, olive oil, and ginger in small bowl. With fork, stir to combine. Set aside.

Wipe shark steaks with damp paper towels. Brush one side of each steak with oil that has risen to the top of sauce. Arrange fish, oiled-sided down, in center of disposable broiling pan. Brush top sides with oil. Broil fish 8 to 10 minutes. Do not turn. Fish is done when it flakes easily and is opaque through.

Remove ginger from marinade and purée sauce in food processor or blender. In a small saucepan, bring sauce to a simmer over medium heat. Stirring occasionally, cook for 3 minutes.

Place sour cream in medium-size bowl and gradually add warmed sauce, stirring until blended.

Remove fish from broiler, cover loosely with aluminum foil and keep warm. Add pan juices to the sauce and stir to combine. Place steaks on serving plates and top with a garnish of lime, if desired. Serve sauce separately. *Serves 4.*

NOTE: Bluefin tuna, albacore, swordfish, or catfish may be substituted for shark.

FILLET OF SOLE BONNE FEMME

2 pounds sole fillets
1 cup water
1 cup dry white wine
1 small onion, thinly sliced

½ *lemon, thinly sliced*
  Salt to taste
½ *teaspoon peppercorns*
¼ *cup butter*
 1 *cup sliced fresh mushrooms*
¼ *cup flour*
¾ *cup light cream*
 1 *tablespoon lemon juice*
  Salt and pepper to taste

Preheat broiler. Place water, wine, onion, lemon, salt, and peppercorns in a large saucepan. Bring to a boil over medium heat. Add fillets in a single layer (add boiling water to cover if necessary), and simmer 5 to 7 minutes per inch of thickness.

Remove fillets, drain and place in a lightly greased, shallow baking dish. Strain poaching liquid and return to saucepan. Boil liquid uncovered over high heat until reduced to ¾ cup.

In another saucepan, melt butter over low heat. Add mushrooms and sauté for 3 minutes. Blend in flour. Gradually add strained liquid and cream, stirring over medium heat until thick. Add lemon juice, salt, and pepper. Mix well. Pour over fillets, covering them completely.

Place broiler 5 to 6 inches from heat and cook for 2 to 3 minutes until the sauce starts to brown. *Serves 4.*

FILLETS OF SOLE FLORENTINE

 6 *fillets of sole (about 2½ pounds)*
  Lemon juice
 2 *tablespoons finely chopped shallots*
 2 *teaspoons dried tarragon leaves*
 1 *teaspoon salt*
 1 *cup dry white wine*
 2 *10-ounce packages frozen chopped spinach*
 1 *recipe Wine Sauce*
½ *cup heavy cream*
 1 *recipe Hollandaise Sauce*

Preheat broiler. Rinse fillets under cool water. Pat dry with paper towels. Brush both sides with lemon juice. Fold into thirds,

81

dark side inside. Arrange in a single layer in a large skillet. Sprinkle with shallots, tarragon, and salt. Pour on the wine. Bring just to a boil. Reduce heat, cover, and simmer 5 to 10 minutes or until fish flakes when tested with fork. Do not overcook.

Cook spinach. Turn into sieve and drain, pressing spinach to remove all liquid. Return to saucepan, cover, and keep hot.

With a slotted spatula, lift fillets to heated platter. Keep warm. Strain liquid from skillet into a 2-cup measure. You should have 1 cup liquid; boil it down if necessary. Set aside.

Stir ⅓ cup Wine Sauce into drained spinach; toss. Spread mixture evenly into a 12-by-8-by-2-inch broiler-proof serving dish. Arrange fillets in a single layer on spinach. Spoon remaining Wine Sauce over them. Beat heavy cream until stiff. Fold it into cooled Hollandaise Sauce and spoon over all. Place under broiler 2 to 3 minutes, or until top turns a golden brown. Serve immediately. *Serves 6.*

WINE SAUCE

> 3 tablespoons butter or margarine
> 3 tablespoons flour
> Salt to taste
> ⅛ teaspoon pepper
> 1 cup fish and wine stock (from preparation of fillets)
> ⅓ cup light cream

Melt butter in a medium-sized saucepan. Remove from heat and stir in flour, salt, and pepper. Gradually stir in the cup of reserved fish and wine stock and light cream. Return to medium heat and bring to a boil, stirring constantly until mixture thickens. Remove from heat and use immediately. *Makes 1½ cups.*

HOLLANDAISE SAUCE

> 3 egg yolks
> ½ cup, or 1 stick, lightly salted butter, frozen
> 1 tablespoon water
> 2 tablespoons lemon juice
> ⅛ teaspoon salt

Combine egg yolks, frozen butter, water, lemon juice, and salt in a heavy saucepan. Stir over medium heat with a wire whisk until butter melts and sauce is smooth. Remove from heat before it becomes too thick. Cool completely. *Makes 1 cup.*

SINKER TUNA WITH ORANGE-CUMIN SAUCE

4 ³⁄₄-inch-thick fillets of bluefin tuna, yellowtail, or mackerel
¼ cup cumin seeds
1 cup fresh orange juice
1 tablespoon dark brown sugar
¼ cup virgin olive oil
1 orange, thinly sliced, for garnish, optional
   Parsley sprigs, for garnish, optional

Preheat broiler. In a small, dry, heavy skillet, toast cumin seeds over medium heat for about 2 minutes, or until fragrance is released. Shake skillet from time to time to keep seeds from scorching. Grind seeds with mortar and pestle or place between 2 sheets of waxed paper and crush with a rolling pin.

Combine juice, cumin, and brown sugar in a small saucepan. Bring to a boil over high heat. Cook for about 5 minutes or until sauce is reduced to ½ cup. Set aside and keep warm.

Wipe tuna fillets with damp paper towels. Place fillets in broiling pan and brush on both sides with olive oil. Broil 4 to 5 inches from heat, 3 to 4 minutes per side or until just done.

Remove from heat and transfer fillets to warm platter. Top each with sauce. Garnish platter with orange slices and parsley sprigs, if desired. *Serves 4.*

MIDDLE EAST FISH STEW

12 mussels
½ pound medium-size fresh shrimp
1 pound whole king or Spanish mackerel, boned
2 squid, cleaned and cut into rings (about 1 pound total weight)
6 tablespoons olive oil
2 large yellow onions, sliced
1 fennel bulb, sliced (or 1 tablespoon fennel seeds)
6 cloves garlic, minced
1 teaspoon saffron threads, crushed
½ cup white Burgundy wine
1 32-ounce can Italian plum tomatoes
¼ cup tomato paste
1 tablespoon chopped fresh basil (or 1 teaspoon dried)
2 tablespoons grated orange rind
2 tablespoons chopped fresh parsley, for garnish, optional

With stiff brush, scrub mussels under cold running water. Pull off beards. Shell and devein shrimp. Cut mackerel into 1½-inch pieces. Set aside.

In large stockpot, heat oil over medium-high heat until hot but not smoking. Add onions and fresh fennel, if available. Sauté, stirring with a wooden spoon until onions are soft but not transparent, about 5 minutes. Add garlic, saffron, and wine. Cook 1 minute.

Add tomatoes, tomato paste, basil, and fennel seed, if using. Break up tomatoes with spoon. Cover, reduce heat to low and cook 30 minutes. Stir in orange rind.

Add mussels to tomato mixture and cook 2 minutes. Add shrimp and squid, then gently top with fish pieces. Cook 3 minutes. Turn off heat.

When ready to serve, gently ladle stew into serving bowl so that fish pieces do not fall apart. If desired, garnish with chopped parsley. *Serves 4.*

SEAFOOD COQUILLES

1 *pound mixed cooked seafood of your choice*
½ *cup water*
½ *cup dry white wine*
4 *thin slices onion*
4 *thin slices lemon*
2 *sprigs parsley*
1 *bay leaf*
6 *peppercorns*
  Salt to taste
2 *tablespoons butter*
¼ *cup sliced mushrooms*
2 *tablespoons flour*
¼ *cup light cream*
¼ *cup bread crumbs*
2 *tablespoons grated cheddar cheese*

Preheat oven to 500°. Bring water and wine to a boil with onion, lemon, parsley, bay leaf, peppercorns, and salt. Strain and reserve the broth.

In a saucepan, over medium heat, melt the butter. Sauté the mushrooms for 5 minutes. Blend in flour and slowly add reserved broth, stirring constantly over medium heat until thick. Add cream and fold in seafood. Pour into 4 or 6 greased scallop shells.

Bake at 500° for 5 to 8 minutes or until bubbly. Remove from heat. Mix bread crumbs with cheese, then sprinkle over the seafood. Place under broiler for 1 to 2 minutes or until golden brown. *Serves 2 to 3 people as an entrée; 4 to 6 as an appetizer.*

NOTE: Try crab or shrimp, or fillet of salmon, halibut, cod or turbot, cut into cubes.

SEAFOOD CURRY CHOWDER

1 fillet of halibut, scrod, or cod (about 8 ounces)
1 fillet of flounder (about 8 ounces)
½ pound medium-size shrimp, shelled and deveined (10 to 12)
2 tablespoons lemon juice
4 tablespoons unsalted butter
¼ cup flour
Curry powder to taste, but at least 1 teaspoon
2 cups Court Bouillon (see page 19) or clam juice
2 cups chicken stock
Salt and pepper to taste
½ cup frozen petite peas, thawed
½ cup heavy cream
2 tablespoons finely chopped fresh dill

Wipe fish fillets with damp paper towel. Cut halibut into ½-inch pieces. Cut flounder into ¾-inch pieces. Cut shrimp in half lengthwise. Place fish and shrimp in a medium-size bowl, sprinkle with lemon juice and toss to combine. Set aside.

In large, heavy saucepan, melt butter over medium-low heat. Add flour and curry powder to taste. Whisk until thoroughly blended. Cook, stirring constantly, 3 minutes. Continue whisking, slowly adding Court Bouillon (or clam juice) and chicken stock. Add salt and pepper and, stirring occasionally, bring to a boil over medium-high heat. Reduce heat; cover and simmer 10 minutes.

Add fish and shrimp, peas, and cream; stir to combine. Simmer for 5 minutes.

Remove pan from heat and whisk in dill.

Ladle chowder into individual soup bowls and serve immediately. *Serves 4 to 6.*

Chapter Two

Sharon Anderson

UPLAND BIRDS

MENU

❧

Pheasant
with Avocado Pomegranate Sauce

Buttered Noodles

Poysippi Glazed Carrots

Romaine and Red Onion Salad
with Manion Vinaigrette

Angel Food Cake
with Chocolate Whipped Cream

PHEASANT WITH AVOCADO POMEGRANATE SAUCE

    1   2½-pound pheasant
    ¼   cup peanut oil
    1½ cups cooked tomatoes
    1   cup chicken broth
    ¼   teaspoon ground cloves
    ¼   teaspoon pepper
    ¼   teaspoon cinnamon
        Pinch of saffron
    ¼   cup blanched almonds
    ¼   cup raisins
    1   cup Malaga wine
    2   slices white bread, if needed
        Seeds of one pomegranate
    1   avocado, peeled and sliced

Disjoint bird. Fry in hot oil in a Dutch oven over medium heat for about 30 minutes or until browned on both sides. Add tomatoes, broth, spices, almonds, and raisins. Cover, reduce heat, and simmer until meat is tender and sauce thick. Add wine and simmer 5 minutes more. If sauce is runny, grind 1 or 2 slices of white bread in blender and add for thickening. Remove pheasant to platter. Pour sauce over bird and sprinkle with pomegranate seeds. Garnish with avocado slices. Serve with buttered noodles. *Serves 4.*

POYSIPPI GLAZED CARROTS

3 cups sliced cooked carrots
1½ cups unsweetened pineapple juice
2 tablespoons lemon juice
1 teaspoon grated lemon rind
½ teaspoon grated orange rind
2 tablespoons sugar
2 tablespoons cornstarch

Combine all ingredients, except cornstarch, in a saucepan over medium heat. Bring to a boil. Stir in 2 tablespoons cornstarch diluted with a bit of cold water. Lower heat and continue cooking until sauce is thick. Serve immediately. *Serves 4.*

ROMAINE AND RED ONION SALAD

1 small head romaine lettuce, washed, dried, and torn into bite-size pieces
1 large red onion, sliced
½ cup herbed croutons
1 recipe Manion Vinaigrette (see page 40)

Toss all ingredients together, making sure that the onion slices break into rings. Serve immediately. *Serves 4.*

ANGEL FOOD CAKE WITH CHOCOLATE WHIPPED CREAM

11 *egg whites*
 1 *teaspoon cream of tartar*
 1 *cup cake flour*
1½ *cups superfine sugar*
 1 *teaspoon vanilla extract*
 1 *recipe Chocolate Whipped Cream*

Preheat oven to 375°. Beat egg whites with cream of tartar until very stiff but not dry. Sift the flour and sugar together twice and gently fold into the egg whites ¼ cup at a time. *Do not overmix.* Fold in vanilla.

Pour into ungreased 9-inch tube or angel food cake pan. Bake at 375° for 50 minutes or until cake is high and golden. Remove from oven and cool upside down, allowing room underneath for air to circulate.

When cool, carefully remove from pan by running a knife along edges. To serve, slice with a serrated knife or pull apart with two forks. Serve with chocolate whipped cream. *Serves 8.*

CHOCOLATE WHIPPED CREAM

1 *cup heavy cream*
1 *tablespoon unsweetened cocoa powder*
2 *tablespoons confectioners' sugar*

Beat all ingredients together until very thick, but not stiff. Use immediately. *Serves 8.*

MENU

❧

Country Inn Hearty Pheasant

Scalloped Potatoes

*Spinach Salad
with Sage Sauce*

Washington Apple Cake

COUNTRY INN HEARTY PHEASANT

6 whole boneless, skinless pheasant breasts, cut in half
⅓ cup butter
⅓ cup plus 1 tablespoon flour
12 thin slices ham
6 1-ounce slices mild cheese
¼ cup chopped shallots
3 large cloves garlic, minced
½ pound mushrooms, sliced
½ cup dry white wine
1 cup chicken broth
1 teaspoon oregano
1 teaspoon thyme
½ cup dry sherry or cream sherry
½ cup cream
    Salt and pepper to taste

Preheat oven to 375°. Melt butter in a heavy skillet over medium heat. Dredge pheasant in ⅓ cup flour and fry until lightly browned on both sides. Arrange in a buttered 13-by-9-by-2-inch baking dish. Top each piece with 1 slice ham and ½ slice cheese. In the skillet, sauté shallots and garlic until soft. Add mushrooms, wine, broth, and herbs. Bring to a boil. Lower heat and cook 10 minutes. Stir 1 tablespoon flour and a small amount of sherry into simmering sauce. When blended, stir in remaining sherry and cream. Season with salt and pepper to taste. Pour sauce over pheasant. Bake at 375° for 20 minutes. *Serves 6.*

SCALLOPED POTATOES

6 large Idaho potatoes, peeled and thinly sliced
Salt and pepper to taste
Approximately ½ cup butter
Milk to cover

Preheat oven to 375°. Generously butter a medium-size casserole. Arrange a layer of potatoes on the bottom. Sprinkle with salt and pepper and dot with butter. Keep layering until all potatoes are used. Pour on just enough milk to cover potatoes.

Cover and place in a 375° oven. Bake for 30 minutes. Remove cover and continue baking for about 15 minutes or until potatoes are done and top is light brown. Remove from oven and serve immediately. *Serves 6.*

SPINACH SALAD WITH SAGE SAUCE

½ cup finely chopped fresh spinach, stems removed
½ cup finely chopped watercress, stems removed
¼ cup finely chopped fresh parsley
1 teaspoon crushed dried sage
¼ teaspoon black pepper
1 tablespoon lemon juice
1 cup Homemade Mayonnaise
20 large spinach leaves, torn into bite-size pieces

Mix first six ingredients into 1 cup Homemade Mayonnaise. Refrigerate, covered, overnight. Serve ⅓ cup chopped salad on a bed of fresh spinach leaves. *Serves 6.*

HOMEMADE MAYONNAISE

2 *teaspoons salt*
1 *teaspoon dry mustard*
 Dash of cayenne
2 *egg yolks*
1 *pint olive or salad oil*
2 *tablespoons cider vinegar*
2 *tablespoons tarragon vinegar*

Combine dry ingredients with unbeaten egg yolks in a mixing bowl. Beat together until stiff. Add the oil, beating it into the mixture drop by drop, then pouring more rapidly, always keeping the mixture stiff. When it begins to thicken, add a small amount of vinegar. Alternate oil and vinegar until blended. Cover and refrigerate until ready to use. *Makes 2½ cups.*

WASHINGTON APPLE CAKE

2 *cups sifted cake flour*
¼ *teaspoon salt*
1 *teaspoon baking soda*
1 *teaspoon baking powder*
½ *cup butter*
1 *cup sugar*
2 *eggs*
1½ *tablespoons sour milk*
1 *cup cored, shredded, unpeeled apples*
¼ *cup broken nut meats*
1 *teaspoon vanilla*
1 *recipe Caramel Icing*

Preheat oven to 350°. Sift flour, salt, baking soda, and baking powder together. Set aside. Cream butter with sugar until fluffy. Add eggs and beat thoroughly. Add sifted dry ingredients, milk, and apples alternately in small amounts, beating well after each addition. Add remaining ingredients, mixing lightly. Pour into greased 8-by-4-inch loaf pan and bake at 350° for about 1 hour or until a knife inserted in center comes out clean. Remove from pan and cool on wire rack. Frost entire cake, when cool, with Caramel Icing. When icing is firm, store covered in a cool, dry place. May be kept several days. *Serves 8.*

CARAMEL ICING

2 *cups brown sugar*
1 *cup granulated sugar*
⅛ *teaspoon baking soda*
¾ *cup cream*
1 *egg white*

Combine sugars, baking soda, and cream in a heavy saucepan. Cook, stirring constantly, to 238° on a candy thermometer, or until a small amount forms a soft ball when dropped into cold water. Cool to lukewarm without stirring. Beat until creamy, add unbeaten egg white and beat until thick enough to spread. May be refrigerated, covered, for up to 1 week. *Makes enough frosting for three 8-inch layers.*

MENU

❦

Royal Celery Soup

*Breast of Pheasant
with Wild Mushroom Duxelles en
Brioche*

Fried Apples

Steamed Asparagus

Brioche Rolls

Fig Banana Brick

ROYAL CELERY SOUP

3 stalks celery, cut into 1-inch pieces
1 thick slice onion
3 cups milk
2 tablespoons butter
2 tablespoons flour
1 teaspoon salt
¼ teaspoon pepper
1 cup cream

Cook celery in top half of double boiler over boiling water with onion and milk for 20 minutes. Remove onion and celery; puree and set aside. Heat the butter in a small saucepan over medium heat. Add flour and seasonings, then ⅔ cup of the milk. Gradually stir in remaining milk. Add cream and celery and onion. Cook until smooth and slightly thick. Serve hot. *Serves 4.*

96

BREAST OF PHEASANT WITH WILD MUSHROOM DUXELLES EN BRIOCHE

1 whole fresh pheasant
  Salt and pepper to taste
3 tablespoons butter
2 tablespoons minced shallots
⅔ cup chopped assorted wild mushrooms
½ clove garlic, minced
1 tablespoon fines herbes
2 tablespoons fresh bread crumbs
1 egg
1 pound spinach leaves, washed, trimmed, and wilted
1 5-by-5-by-⅛-inch square Brioche Dough
1 recipe Sauce Supreme

Preheat oven to 350°. Prepare pheasant by removing breast from carcass. Skin and French (by exposing first wing bone). Season with salt and pepper. Melt 2 tablespoons butter in heavy skillet over medium heat. Brown pheasant on each side. Remove from pan and cool.

Prepare duxelles by sautéing shallots, mushrooms, garlic, and fines herbes in 1 tablespoon butter over medium heat for approximately 10 minutes or until soft. Remove excess liquid; add fresh bread crumbs and egg. Mix to blend. Cool slightly.

Cover pheasant breast with duxelles and wrap with wilted spinach leaves. Wrap in brioche dough. Press edges together and push wing bone through the dough. Make an egg wash with 1 egg whisked with 1 tablespoon milk to hold pastry together. Snip excess dough with scissors. Place on baking sheet and let rest for 15 minutes.

Egg wash top and place in 350° oven for 25 minutes or until brioche dough is golden brown. Remove from heat. Place on serving platter and coat with Sauce Supreme. *Serves 4.*

The author's thanks to Executive Chef Helmut Leuck, of New York City's Grand Hyatt Hotel, for this breast of pheasant recipe.

SAUCE SUPREME

4 tablespoons butter
2 tablespoons flour
2 cups hot chicken broth
2 egg yolks
⅓ cup heavy cream
  Dash of ground nutmeg
  Salt and pepper to taste

Melt 2 tablespoons butter in a small saucepan over low heat. Add 2 tablespoons flour and stir to blend. Whisk in hot chicken broth and cook, stirring constantly, until thick. Mix together egg yolks and cream. Slowly add ½ cup sauce to egg yolks, whisking vigorously. Pour back into the sauce, stirring constantly. Cook over low heat, stirring in 2 tablespoons butter, nutmeg, salt, and pepper to taste. Serve immediately. *Makes 2½ cups.*

BRIOCHE DOUGH

2 cups warm milk
3 ounces brewer's yeast
12 cups bread flour
1 tablespoon salt
¾ cup sugar
24 large egg yolks
2½ cups softened butter

Preheat oven to 375°. Mix together the milk, brewer's yeast, and 4 cups of bread flour. Beat for 4 minutes. Cover and let rest free from drafts until double in size. When doubled, add remaining flour to dough and beat until dough pulls thinly away from ball. Add remaining ingredients and knead for 10 minutes. Cover and let rest, free from drafts, until double in size. Knead and roll into desired shape.

NOTE: Use amount needed for Breast of Pheasant with Wild Mushroom Duxelles en Brioche and form the remaining dough into an equal number of large (approximately 3-inch diameter) and small (approximately 1-inch diameter) balls. Place the large balls in a greased brioche or muffin tin. Make a deep impression in center of each, and place a small ball into it. Allow to rise, covered and free from drafts, until large ball rises to top of tin. Brush with egg wash, bake for 20 minutes at 375° or until the rolls are golden brown. Remove from heat and serve warm. You can also make a large brioche in either a large brioche pan or a casserole following above directions.

FRIED APPLES

4 tablespoons butter
1 teaspoon grated lemon rind
2 tablespoons light brown sugar
½ teaspoon ground cinnamon
    Dash of brandy
3 large Granny Smith apples, cored and sliced ½-inch thick

Place the butter in a heavy skillet over low heat. Add lemon rind, sugar, cinnamon, and brandy. Stir to blend. Add apple slices. Cook, turning occasionally, for about 15 minutes or until apples are golden brown. Serve immediately. *Serves 4.*

FIG BANANA BRICK

2 tablespoons quick-cooking tapioca
1½ cups milk
2 tablespoons sugar
⅛ teaspoon salt
1 cup dried figs
1 cup heavy cream
1 cup mashed bananas
½ teaspoon grated lemon rind
2 teaspoons vanilla

In top half of double boiler, cook tapioca and milk over hot water for 10 minutes. Strain but do not rub tapioca through the sieve. Add sugar and salt to strained milk mixture. Chill. Boil figs for 10 minutes in water to cover. Drain and cool. Clip stems and chop. Whip cream until stiff. Combine with figs, cold milk mixture, bananas, lemon rind, and vanilla. Mix thoroughly. Pour into freezer tray. Freeze, stirring 2 or 3 times. Unmold and slice. Top with whipped cream if desired. *Serves 8.*

MENU

❧

Chester Pheasant in Foil

Maureen Costello Potatoes

Lemon Mushroom Salad

Pineapple Tarts

CHESTER PHEASANT IN FOIL

1 2½-pound pheasant
½ cup melted butter
1½ teaspoons poultry seasoning
½ orange
½ cup dry white wine

Preheat oven to 425°. Brush entire surface of bird with melted butter, and sprinkle cavity and surface of pheasant with poultry seasoning.

Stuff ½ orange in cavity. Place bird on heavy duty aluminum foil. Bring edges together and seal tightly. Place in shallow roasting pan and bake at 425° for 1¼ hours. Open foil and allow pheasant to brown for another 15 minutes. Remove pheasant and foil from pan but leave juices. Add ½ cup dry white wine to drippings and

100

heat to boiling. Cut pheasant into quarters and serve with the clear wine gravy. *Serves 4.*

MAUREEN COSTELLO POTATOES

6 *potatoes, peeled and cubed*
3 *tablespoons butter*
½ *teaspoon salt*
½ *teaspoon paprika*
2 *eggs, well beaten*
¼ *cup grated cheddar cheese*
½ *cup buttered bread crumbs*

Preheat oven to 350°. Cook potatoes in lightly salted water. Drain potatoes and rice. Add butter, seasonings, and eggs to hot riced potatoes. Beat until light. Pile into greased baking dish. Sprinkle with grated cheese and buttered crumbs. Bake at 350° for about 15 minutes or until crumbs are brown. *Serves 4 to 6.*

LEMON MUSHROOM SALAD

1 *pound fresh mushrooms, sliced ⅛ inch thick*
¼ *cup fresh lemon juice*
½ *cup olive oil*
2 *scallions, thinly sliced*
¼ *cup chopped fresh parsley*
1 *clove garlic, minced*
 Salt to taste
¼ *teaspoon freshly ground black pepper*
½ *pound fresh spinach, washed, dried, and trimmed*
 Parsley sprigs
 Paprika
 Grissini

Toss mushrooms with lemon juice in large bowl. Stir in the next six ingredients. Toss to mix. Cover and refrigerate, tossing once or twice, at least 3 hours but no longer than 24 hours.

For best flavor, bring mushrooms to room temperature. Transfer to serving bowl lined with fresh spinach leaves. Garnish with parsley sprigs and sprinkle with paprika. Serve with grissini. *Serves 4 to 6.*

NOTE: Crunchy grissini (very long, very thin breadsticks) are available in Italian bakeries.

PINEAPPLE TARTS

2 cups canned crushed, unsweetened pineapple, drained
¼ cup maraschino cherries, quartered
2 tablespoons pineapple juice
½ cup sugar
¼ teaspoon grated lemon rind
1 recipe Plain Pastry (see page 8)
2 tablespoons butter

Preheat oven to 425°. Combine first five ingredients. Cut pastry into eight 5-inch squares. Arrange pastry squares in muffin pans and place 3 heaping tablespoons pineapple mixture into each. Dot with butter. Draw corners of pastry over filling. Bake at 425°, for 20 to 25 minutes or until pastry is lightly browned. *Makes 8 tarts.*

MENU

*Briar Patch Pheasant
with Cabbage*

Corn Cakes

Royal Salad

Chess Pie

BRIAR PATCH PHEASANT WITH CABBAGE

1 2½-pound pheasant
1 small cabbage, shredded
2 leeks, sliced
2 medium onions, sliced
2 carrots, sliced
1 small whole onion, peeled
3 slices bacon
  Salt to taste
6 peppercorns
2 tablespoons port wine

Place cabbage in a pot of cold water and bring to a boil. Immediately remove from heat and drain. Line a greased 2-quart casserole with cabbage and top with remaining vegetables. Place the small onion in the cavity of the pheasant. Lay bacon strips across

103

the breast. Place pheasant on top of the vegetables in casserole. Add salt, peppercorns, and port. Cover and simmer, over low heat, for 1½ hours. Remove pheasant and strain cabbage and vegetables. Place pheasant on serving platter and surround with vegetables. Serve immediately. *Serves 4.*

CORN CAKES

1 cup flour
2 tablespoons finely ground cornmeal
2 teaspoons baking powder
¼ teaspoon salt
1 extra large egg
1 cup milk
1 tablespoon melted butter
½ teaspoon fresh minced dill
1 cup whole kernel corn (preferably fresh)
½ cup sour cream, optional

Sift dry ingredients together. Blend in egg and milk. Add melted butter, dill, and corn. Stir to mix.

Heat griddle until very hot. Brush with corn oil. Lower heat to medium high. Pour in enough batter to make 3-inch diameter cakes. When top of cake is bubbly, turn and brown other side. Turn only once.

Keep cakes warm until all are finished. Serve warm with a dollop of sour cream on top. *Makes approximately 16 cakes.*

ROYAL SALAD

4 romaine lettuce leaves
1 orange, peeled and sectioned
1 grapefruit, peeled and sectioned
1 pear, peeled and sliced
1 green pepper, seeded and sliced
1 recipe Strawberry Mayonnaise
4 strawberries

Arrange romaine leaves on individual salad plates. On each plate place 3 segments of orange, 2 of grapefruit, and 2 of pear, separating the different fruits with a slice of green pepper. Cover top with Strawberry Mayonnaise and top with a whole strawberry. *Serves 4.*

STRAWBERRY MAYONNAISE

½ *cup mayonnaise*
½ *cup mashed fresh strawberries*
 1 *teaspoon confectioners' sugar*
 1 *tablespoon lemon juice*
½ *cup whipped cream*

Blend together mayonnaise, mashed strawberries, confectioners' sugar, and lemon juice. Fold in whipped cream. Use immediately. *Makes 1½ cups.*

CHESS PIE

½ *cup butter*
 1 *cup sugar*
 3 *egg yolks*
 1 *egg white*
 1 *cup chopped raisins*
 1 *cup chopped nut meats*
 1 *teaspoon vanilla*
 1 *9-inch unbaked pie shell (see Plain Pastry, page 8)*
 1 *recipe Whipped Cream Topping*

Cream butter and sugar. Add beaten egg yolks and stiffly beaten egg white. Mix well. Add raisins, nuts, and vanilla. Pour into pie shell and bake at 400° for 20 to 24 minutes or until set. Remove from heat. Cool and top with Whipped Cream Topping. *Serves 4 to 8.*

WHIPPED CREAM TOPPING

½ cup heavy cream
¼ cup sugar
1 teaspoon vanilla
¾ teaspoon unflavored gelatin
2 tablespoons milk

Whip cream until almost stiff. Add sugar and vanilla and beat until cream holds a peak.

Sprinkle ¾ teaspoon unflavored gelatin over 2 tablespoons milk and stir thoroughly. Place over boiling water and stir until dissolved. Add to cream which is at room temperature. Chill and whip. *Makes enough topping for one 9-inch pie.*

OTHER RECIPES

PHEASANT BREASTS WITH CINNAMON MARMALADE

2 pheasant breasts, halved, boned, and skin removed
2 tablespoons butter or margarine
4 teaspoons flour
¼ teaspoon ground cinnamon
½ cup orange juice
2 tablespoons orange marmalade
¾ teaspoon instant chicken bouillon
1 tablespoon orange liqueur, optional
½ cup white seedless grapes
1 orange, peeled and cut into sections
¼ cup toasted sliced almonds

Preheat oven to 325°. Line an 8-by-8-by-2-inch baking pan with heavy duty aluminum foil, leaving 1½-inch foil collar. Place pheasant in single layer in pan. Melt butter in saucepan over medium heat. Stir in flour and cinnamon. Cook until smooth. Blend in orange juice, marmalade, and bouillon. Bring to a boil, stirring until thick. Stir in liqueur. Spoon sauce over pheasant. Seal by tightly closing foil collar. Bake at 325° for 30 minutes or until meat is tender. Open foil and spoon grapes and orange sections over pheasant. Bake, uncovered, an additional 5 minutes or until fruit is heated. Remove from heat. Sprinkle with almonds. Serve immediately with rice. *Serves 4.*

MENU

✿

Buttermilk Pecan Quail

*Pepper Casserole
with Mustard*

*German Potato Salad
with Sour Cream*

Vermont Maple Sugar Pound Cake

BUTTERMILK PECAN QUAIL

8 *quail, cut in half*
3/4 *cup butter*
1 *cup buttermilk*
1 *egg, lightly beaten*
1 *cup all-purpose flour*
1 *cup ground pecans*
1/4 *cup sesame seeds*
1 *tablespoon paprika*
  Salt and pepper to taste
1/2 *cup pecan halves*

Preheat oven to 350°. Place butter in large shallow roasting pan and melt in oven. Remove and set aside.

In shallow dish, mix buttermilk and egg. In medium bowl combine flour, ground pecans, sesame seeds, paprika, salt, and pepper.

Coat quail in buttermilk mixture, then in flour mixture. Place in roasting pan, turning to coat all sides with butter, finishing with skin side up. Scatter pecan halves over quail and bake at 350° for 1½ hours or until quail is golden brown. *Serves 8.*

PEPPER CASSEROLE WITH MUSTARD

1½ cups water
1 teaspoon salt
2 packages frozen Fordhook lima beans
2 medium green peppers, cut in ¾-inch julienne strips
¼ pound bacon, cut in ½-inch pieces
1 tablespoon packed brown sugar
1 teaspoon dry mustard
1 tablespoon molasses
2 cups stewed tomatoes

Preheat oven to 325°. Heat water and salt to boiling. Add lima beans and green pepper strips. Bring to a boil. Reduce heat, cover, and simmer until tender, about 8 minutes. Drain vegetables and set aside.

Cook bacon pieces in medium skillet until limp but not brown. Stir in brown sugar, mustard, molasses, and stewed tomatoes. Cook over low heat 5 minutes.

Blend tomatoes and vegetables. Pour into buttered 2-quart casserole. Cover. Bake at 325° 35 to 40 minutes, or until bubbly. *Serves 4 to 6.*

GERMAN POTATO SALAD WITH SOUR CREAM

5 medium potatoes, boiled
1 teaspoon sugar
½ teaspoon salt
¼ teaspoon dry mustard
⅛ teaspoon freshly ground black pepper
2 tablespoons vinegar
1 cup sour cream
½ cup thinly sliced cucumbers
Paprika

Slice potatoes while still warm. If new potatoes are used, slice in their jackets. Other potatoes should be peeled.

Mix the sugar, salt, mustard, pepper, and vinegar. Add the sour cream and cucumber and mix. Pour over the potatoes and toss lightly until all the potatoes have been coated with dressing. Turn into a serving dish and sprinkle with paprika. Serve warm. *Serves 4.*

VERMONT MAPLE SUGAR POUND CAKE

4½ cups sifted all-purpose flour
½ teaspoon salt
1 cup softened butter
2 cups maple sugar
10 eggs (at room temperature)
1 teaspoon vanilla extract
½ teaspoon lemon extract

Preheat oven to 300°. Combine the sifted flour with salt. Sift together several times and set aside. Beat the butter until it is light and fluffy. Add sugar a little at a time, creaming the mixture well after each addition.

Separate the eggs. Beat the yolks until they are thick and pale yellow. Add the yolks to the creamed butter and sugar, and beat until the mixture is light.

Blend in the sifted flour, ½ cup at a time, beating well after each addition. Stir in the flavorings. Beat the egg whites until they form stiff peaks, then gently fold into the batter. Grease and flour two 9¼-by-5¼-by-2¾-inch loaf pans. Divide the batter between them. Bake for about 1 hour and 35 minutes, or until the cakes shrink from the sides of the pans and the top of each loaf springs back when lightly pressed with the fingers. Cool for 15 minutes in the pans before gently removing the cakes to a wire rack to cool further. *Makes two loaves.*

MENU

❧

Quail Baked in Wine

Willow Creek Potato Soufflé

Hearts of Artichoke Salad

Strawberry Shortcake

QUAIL BAKED IN WINE

8 *quail, cleaned and trussed*
½ *cup butter*
1 *cup minced onion*
2 *whole cloves*
1 *teaspoon peppercorns*
2 *cloves garlic, minced*
½ *bay leaf*
2 *cups dry white wine*
 Salt and pepper to taste
 Sprinkle of cayenne pepper
1 *teaspoon minced chives*
2 *cups cream*

Melt butter in heavy skillet over medium heat. Add onions, cloves, peppercorns, garlic, and bay leaf; sauté for 5 minutes. Add quail and brown on all sides. Add wine, salt, pepper, cayenne, and chives. Simmer, covered, until tender, about 30 minutes. Remove quail to hot serving dish. Strain sauce. Add cream and heat to boiling. Immediately pour over quail. *Serves 4.*

WILLOW CREEK POTATO SOUFFLÉ

3 medium potatoes, peeled and quartered
¾ cup heavy cream
  Salt to taste
  Generous pinch of cayenne
¼ cup grated Parmesan cheese
¼ teaspoon oregano
1 tablespoon minced fresh dill
3 egg yolks
4 egg whites

Preheat oven to 375°. Place the potatoes in a large saucepan. Cover with salted water and bring to a boil. Cook, covered, over low heat, until the potatoes are tender. Drain the potatoes. Mash well and stir in ¼ cup of cream. Season with salt and cayenne. Place the mashed potatoes in a saucepan. Add the remaining cream and cook over low heat, stirring constantly, until the mixture is heated through. Remove from the heat and stir in the cheese, oregano, and dill.

Beat in the egg yolks one at a time, beating after each addition until well blended. Cool to room temperature. Beat the egg whites until they are stiff but not dry and fold them into the potato mixture. Pour into a well-buttered 1-quart soufflé dish. Fill two-thirds full.

Bake at 375° for 30 minutes or until high and golden. Serve immediately. *Serves 4.*

HEARTS OF ARTICHOKE SALAD

1 small head romaine, torn into bite-size pieces
1 cup fresh spinach, torn into bite-size pieces
1 cup radish slices
½ cup chopped celery
2 tablespoons chopped shallots

1 recipe Dressing
2 hard-boiled eggs, sliced
1 can (14 ounces) artichoke hearts, drained and quartered (marinated artichoke hearts can be substituted)
Freshly ground pepper

Toss romaine, spinach, radish slices, celery, and shallots with Dressing. Garnish with egg slices and artichoke hearts. Sprinkle with freshly ground pepper. *Serves 4.*

DRESSING

1/4 cup vegetable oil
2 tablespoons apple cider vinegar
2 cloves garlic, crushed
1 teaspoon seasoned salt
1/4 teaspoon salt

Shake all ingredients together in tightly covered jar. Refrigerate until ready to use. *Serves 4.*

STRAWBERRY SHORTCAKE

4 cups sifted flour
6 tablespoons baking powder
2 tablespoons granulated sugar
1 cup vegetable shortening
1 1/4 cups milk
2 eggs, beaten
1 tablespoon melted butter
2 teaspoons confectioners' sugar
1 cup heavy cream, whipped
1/2 teaspoon vanilla
4 cups strawberries, cleaned and hulled
1/2 cup granulated sugar

Preheat oven to 425°. Sift first 3 ingredients. Cut in shortening with 2 knives or pastry blender. Add milk and eggs; knead lightly and divide in half. Place on lightly floured board and pat into shape to fit round pan. Place first layer in pan, brush top with melted butter and place second layer over it. Bake at 425° for 20 minutes or until slightly golden on edges.

Fold confectioners' sugar into whipped cream and vanilla. Reserve a few choice strawberries for garnish. Crush remaining berries and combine with granulated sugar. Separate shortcake layers, spread with whipped cream and top with crushed strawberries. Replace top layer and spread with whipped cream. Arrange whole berries over top. *Serves 4 to 8.*

MENU

❦

Quail/Doves Tarragon
with Wild Rice

Baked Stuffed Cucumbers

Cranberry Ring

Scrumptious Creme Cake

QUAIL/DOVES TARRAGON

   5 *doves, halved*
   6 *½-pound quails, halved*
   2 *medium onions, peeled and chopped*
1½ *pounds sliced mushrooms*
   1 *cup butter*
   1 *cup dry white wine*
   2 *11-ounce cans cream of chicken soup*
   1 *tablespoon fresh onion juice*
  ½ *teaspoon minced fresh tarragon*

Preheat oven to 325°. Sauté chopped onions and mushrooms in ¼ cup butter over medium heat until brown. Add wine. Raise heat and boil 2 minutes. Set aside and keep warm.

Melt remaining butter in a heavy skillet over medium heat. Brown birds on all sides. Remove from skillet and place in baking dish. Add butter from skillet and bake, at 325° for 25 minutes. Combine the soup, onion juice, and tarragon with the sautéed vegetables. Ladle over birds. Cover and return to oven for 30 minutes or until fork tender. Baste birds frequently while baking. Serve hot over wild rice. *Serves 4.*

BAKED STUFFED CUCUMBERS

3 large cucumbers
1 medium onion, chopped
¾ cup bread crumbs
½ cup plus 2 teaspoons butter, melted
Salt and pepper to taste
Bread crumbs
Paprika

Preheat oven to 300°. Halve two cucumbers, then cut lengthwise, making four "boats." Lengthwise, cut a slice from the top of each boat. With a melon ball cutter or teaspoon, scoop out the pulp, being careful to leave a wall of about ¼ inch around sides, including the cut end.

Peel the remaining cucumber, add to the pulp and chop to medium fine. Add onion and place in a colander or strainer to drain well. When drained, add the bread crumbs, ½ cup butter, salt, and pepper. Mix well. Stuff the cucumber boats with the mixture, rounding the tops. Sprinkle bread crumbs over tops. Spoon remaining melted butter over the crumbs and dust with paprika. Place the boats in a shallow baking pan. Add water to cover the bottom of the pan and bake at 300° for 1 hour. Serve immediately. *Serves 4.*

CRANBERRY RING

1 can crushed pineapple
1 tablespoon unflavored gelatin
1 box lemon jelly powder
1 cup ground raw cranberries
Rind of 1 orange, grated

Drain pineapple. Add enough water to pineapple juice to make 2 cups liquid. Pour over gelatin and jelly powder. Stir until dissolved. Add cranberries, pineapple, and orange rind. Pour into lightly oiled 1-quart mold. Cover and refrigerate until set. When set, unmold and serve on a bed of butter lettuce, if desired. *Serves 4 to 6.*

SCRUMPTIOUS CREME CAKE

1¼ cups all-purpose flour
1 cup sugar
1½ teaspoons baking powder
¾ teaspoon ground cardamom
½ teaspoon salt
¾ cup milk
⅓ cup shortening
1 egg
1 teaspoon vanilla
¼ cup water
2 tablespoons granulated sugar
⅓ cup dark rum (or 1 tablespoon rum flavoring)
½ cup finely chopped raisins
1 package (3¼ ounces) vanilla pudding and pie filling
⅓ cup flaked coconut
¼ cup toasted sliced almonds

Preheat oven to 350°. Place flour, 1 cup sugar, baking powder, cardamom, salt, milk, shortening, egg, and vanilla in large bowl. Blend for 30 seconds on low speed of electric mixer, scraping bowl constantly. Beat 3 minutes at high speed, scraping bowl occasionally. Pour into greased and floured 8-by-8-by-2-inch or 9-by-9-by-2-inch pan. Bake at 350° for 45 to 55 minutes, until wooden toothpick inserted in center comes out clean. Remove from pan and cool on wire rack.

Heat water and 2 tablespoons granulated sugar until sugar dissolves. Stir in rum and raisins. Remove from heat. Let stand at least 30 minutes.

Prepare pudding according to package directions, except use only 1½ cups milk. Stir in coconut; let cool.

Split cake horizontally to make 2 layers. Remove raisins from rum mixture. Reserve liquid. Stir raisins into cooled pudding mixture. Prick each layer on cut side with long-tined fork. Drizzle rum over pricked cake. Spread half of the raisin-coconut pudding over bottom layer. Replace top layer. Spread remaining raisin-coconut pudding on top of cake. Press in sliced almonds. Refrigerate, covered, at least 8 hours, but no longer than 24 hours. *Serves 4 to 6.*

MENU

❧

Woodcock
with Wine and Grapes

Risotto

Steamed Broccoli
with Hollandaise Sauce (see page 82)

Grandmother's Old-Fashioned Tarts

WOODCOCK WITH WINE AND GRAPES

10 *woodcocks or doves*
 4 *strips bacon*
 1 *cup flour*
   Salt and pepper to taste
 1 *cup chicken broth*
 1 *cup sauterne wine*
 1 *stalk celery, cut in half*
 3 *carrots, thinly sliced*
½ *cup cooked, sliced mushrooms*
 2 *cups seedless grapes*
½ *cup orange juice*

Preheat oven to 325°. Fry the bacon over medium heat until it is half cooked. Remove bacon and reserve the drippings. Dredge the woodcock in flour seasoned with salt and pepper and sauté in

119

the bacon drippings. Arrange woodcock in a baking dish. Place a small piece of bacon across each breast. Add the broth, wine, celery stalk, and carrots. Cover and bake at 325° for 20 minutes. Add the mushrooms and grapes. Cover and return to oven for 15 minutes. Add orange juice. Cover and bake for 15 minutes more. Remove from heat. Discard the celery. Place birds on warm serving platter. Cover with sauce and serve immediately. *Serves 4.*

RISOTTO

4 tablespoons olive oil
2 tablespoons minced fresh parsley
2 teaspoons minced onion
1 cup rice, uncooked
3 cups chicken broth
 Salt and pepper to taste

Preheat oven to 375°. Heat olive oil in heavy skillet over medium heat. Add parsley and onion. Sauté for 5 minutes. Stir in rice, lower heat and sauté for 5 minutes. Add chicken broth and salt and pepper to taste. Bring to a boil. Remove from heat and pour into a casserole.

Bake at 375° for about 25 minutes or until rice has absorbed all liquid and is tender. Serve immediately. *Serves 4.*

GRANDMOTHER'S OLD-FASHIONED TARTS

1¼ cup steamed sweetened prunes or dates
¼ cup walnut pieces
¼ cup orange juice
1 recipe Plain Pastry (see page 8)

Preheat oven to 450°. Pit prunes or dates and chop fine. Add nut meats and orange juice. Roll pastry ⅛-inch thick and cut into rounds 3½ inches in diameter. Place 1 teaspoon of filling on each. Fold in half, moisten edges and press together. Prick top to allow for escape of steam. Bake on ungreased cookie sheet at 450° for 15 minutes or until golden. *Makes about 12 tarts.*

MENU

Spring Green Turkey Hash

Holiday Tomatoes

Marinated Cauliflower Salad

Apple Orchard Tapioca

SPRING GREEN TURKEY HASH

2½ cups diced cooked dark meat turkey
1½ cups diced cooked white meat turkey
 ½ cup butter
 ¼ teaspoon paprika
 ⅛ cup chopped onions
 1 cup finely diced boiled red potatoes
   Salt and pepper to taste
 ¼ cup chopped fresh parsley
 1 recipe Mustard Sauce

Melt butter in a medium skillet over low heat. Stir in paprika. Mix turkey, onions, and potatoes together. Add salt and pepper to taste. Put mixture into the skillet; pack firmly. Cover skillet and raise heat to medium. Cook 5 to 7 minutes or until edges brown,

121

adding more butter if necessary. Turn out onto a heated plate. Garnish with chopped parsley. Serve hot with Mustard Sauce. *Serves 4.*

MUSTARD SAUCE

½ cup Dijon mustard
2 tablespoons yellow mustard
3 cups chicken broth
½ cup beef broth
2 tablespoons butter, softened
2 tablespoons flour

Combine Dijon mustard, yellow mustard, and chicken and beef broths in a small saucepan over medium heat. Blend butter and flour together, and whisk into the mustard sauce. Stir until sauce is the consistency of heavy cream. Serve immediately over turkey hash. *Makes approximately 4 cups.*

HOLIDAY TOMATOES

4 ripe tomatoes
4 tablespoons olive oil
2 tablespoons flour
1 tablespoon sugar
⅛ teaspoon ground nutmeg
   Salt and pepper to taste
½ cup dry bread crumbs
4 tablespoons butter

Wash tomatoes and cut into ½-inch slices. Dip tomato slices in oil and sprinkle lightly on both sides with mixture of flour, sugar, and seasonings. Dip again into oil, then into the bread crumbs.

Melt butter in a heavy skillet over medium heat. Brown tomatoes on each side and serve immediately. *Serves 4.*

Marinated Cauliflower Salad

1 head cauliflower, cored and sliced
1 cup chopped pitted green olives
1 green pepper, cut in thin julienne strips
¼ cup chopped pimento
1 medium onion, finely chopped
½ cup salad oil
   Juice of ½ lemon
3 teaspoons white wine vinegar
   Salt and pepper to taste
½ teaspoon sugar

Place all vegetables in a salad bowl. Add remaining ingredients, tossing well until blended. Cover and refrigerate for at least 2 hours, tossing occasionally to mix. Serve on a bed of lettuce, if desired. *Serves 4 to 6.*

NOTE: This salad is even better when marinated for a day or two. May be kept, refrigerated, for up to ten days.

Apple Orchard Tapioca

2½ cups boiling water
½ teaspoon salt
⅓ cup quick-cooking tapioca
1½ pounds medium cooking apples, peeled and cored
½ cup sugar
2 tablespoons butter

Preheat oven to 350°. Add boiling water and salt to tapioca. Cook in top half of double boiler over boiling water until transparent. Arrange apples in buttered pudding dish. Fill cavities with sugar. Pour in tapioca. Dot with butter. Bake at 350° for 45 minutes or until apples are soft. Serve warm with brown sugar and cream.

You may also use sliced or quartered apples, if desired. *Serves 4 to 6.*

MENU

❧

Waupaca Grouse

Baked Onion Rings and Cheese

Avocado Salad
with Frozen Tomato Mayonnaise

Glazed Bartlett Pears

WAUPACA GROUSE

2 2½-pound grouse, split in half
   Salt and pepper to taste
¼ teaspoon ground thyme
¼ teaspoon ground tarragon
¼ cup melted butter
2 tablespoons Dijon mustard
4 teaspoons bread crumbs
4 broiled tomato halves
4 strips crisp bacon

Preheat broiler. Place grouse on broiler rack. Season with salt, pepper, thyme, and tarragon. Brush with melted butter and broil 15 minutes on each side, frequently basting with butter. Remove from broiling rack and pour pan drippings into a bowl. Whisk Dijon

124

mustard into the drippings and spread over grouse. Press bread crumbs over all. Bake at 400° for about 10 minutes or until golden brown. Remove from heat and garnish with a broiled tomato and a bacon strip. Serve immediately. *Serves 4.*

BAKED ONION RINGS AND CHEESE

6 *slices toast, buttered*
3 *cups onion rings, blanched*
¼ *pound American or cheddar cheese, grated*
1 *egg, lightly beaten*
1 *cup milk*
  Salt and pepper to taste
1 *tablespoon butter*
  Paprika

Preheat oven to 375°. Place 3 slices of buttered toast in bottom of a medium-size baking pan. Cover with a layer of 1½ cups onions, then with half the cheese. Repeat. In a small bowl, combine egg, milk, salt, and pepper. Pour over contents of baking pan. Dot with butter and sprinkle with paprika. Bake at 375° for 30 to 35 minutes or until bubbly. *Serves 4.*

AVOCADO SALAD WITH FROZEN TOMATO MAYONNAISE

2 *avocados, peeled and halved*
  Salt
2 *tablespoons lemon juice*
1 *recipe Frozen Tomato Mayonnaise*
  Watercress

Sprinkle avocados with salt and lemon juice. Fill centers with Frozen Tomato Mayonnaise and serve on watercress. *Serves 4.*

FROZEN TOMATO MAYONNAISE

4 tomatoes, peeled, seeded, and finely chopped
1 teaspoon minced onion
1 cup mayonnaise
1/8 teaspoon salt
    Dash of cayenne

Combine all ingredients. Pour into freezer container, cover, and freeze without stirring. Serve, frozen, as a salad dressing in the center of an avocado half, with cold seafood or cold steamed vegetables. May be kept, frozen, for up to 3 months. *Makes approximately 3 cups.*

GLAZED BARTLETT PEARS

8 pear halves, freshly poached or canned
1/4 cup melted butter
1/2 cup maple or dark brown sugar
1/4 teaspoon ground cinnamon
1/8 teaspoon ground cloves
1 tablespoon lemon juice

Preheat oven to 450°. Dip pears in melted butter and arrange in shallow baking pan. Sprinkle remaining ingredients on top. Bake at 450° for about 15 minutes or until brown. *Serves 4.*

MENU

*New Year's Partridge
with Champagne Sauce*

Mashed Potatoes and Parsnips

Steamed Kale

Apple and Nut Salad (see page 52)

Chocolate Nut Cake

NEW YEAR'S PARTRIDGE WITH CHAMPAGNE SAUCE

8 partridge breasts
1 egg, beaten
¼ teaspoon celery salt
1 cup flour
½ cup butter
1 recipe Champagne Sauce

Combine egg and celery salt. Dip partridge in egg and dredge in flour, shaking off the excess. In a heavy skillet over medium heat melt the butter. Sauté the partridge for 6 to 7 minutes on each side, browning well. Set aside and keep warm. *Serves 8.*

CHAMPAGNE SAUCE

½ *cup plus 2 tablespoons butter*
½ *cup flour*
1½ *cups partridge stock*
  Split dry champagne
1 *pint shucked oysters*
½ *cup heavy cream*
2 *egg yolks*
  Salt and pepper to taste

In a large saucepan over medium heat, melt ½ cup butter. Stir in flour. Gradually add partridge stock and whisk until thick. Add champagne and simmer, gently, 30 minutes or until sauce is thick and reduced by half. Add oysters and cook 5 minutes longer.

In a small bowl, beat together cream, remaining 2 tablespoons butter, and egg yolks. Mix a small amount of the hot sauce into the cream, then blend into the remaining sauce. Season to taste with salt and pepper. Ladle sauce over breasts and serve immediately. *Serves 8.*

MASHED POTATOES AND PARSNIPS

6 *medium potatoes, peeled and cubed*
4 *large parsnips, peeled and sliced*
¼ *cup chopped onion*
½ *cup butter*
⅓ *cup hot milk*
  Salt and pepper to taste
  Dash of ground nutmeg
¼ *cup melted butter*

Cook potatoes, parsnips, and onion in salted water, covered, for about 20 minutes or until very tender. Remove from heat and drain. Place in bowl with remaining ingredients, except butter, and whip until light and fluffy. Serve immediately with melted butter poured over top. *Serves 8.*

STEAMED KALE

4 pounds kale, well washed and trimmed
2 tablespoons butter, melted
1 tablespoon fresh lemon juice
3 drops Tabasco
 Salt and pepper to taste
1 hard-boiled egg yolk, sieved

Place well washed kale in a large pot. Do not add water (water remaining on leaves will provide enough moisture). Cover and cook over low heat for about 3 minutes or until thoroughly wilted. Remove from heat and drain. Toss with butter, lemon juice, and Tabasco. Add salt and pepper to taste. Sprinkle with egg yolk and serve immediately. *Serves 8.*

CHOCOLATE NUT CAKE

1¾ cups sifted cake flour
 2 teaspoons baking powder
 ½ teaspoon ground cloves
 ½ teaspoon ground cinnamon
 ½ teaspoon ground allspice
 ¾ cup butter
1½ cups sugar
 4 eggs, separated
 4 ounces unsweetened chocolate, melted
 1 cup milk
 1 cup chopped walnut meats
 1 teaspoon vanilla
 1 recipe Marshmallow Icing

Preheat oven to 325°. Sift flour, baking powder, and spices together 3 times. Cream butter and sugar until fluffy. Add egg yolks and chocolate. Beat vigorously. Add sifted dry ingredients and milk, alternately, in small amounts, beating well after each addition. Stir in nuts and vanilla. Beat egg whites until stiff, but not dry, and fold into batter. Pour into greased 8-by-4-inch loaf pan and bake at 325°

129

about 50 minutes or until cake tests done. Remove from oven and unmold. Cool on wire rack. When cool, spread top and sides with Marshmallow Icing. *Serves 6 to 8.*

MARSHMALLOW ICING

1¼ *cups sugar*
¼ *cup light corn syrup*
    Dash of salt
¼ *cup water*
 1 *egg white, stiffly beaten*
½ *teaspoon vanilla*
 4 *marshmallows*

Cook sugar, corn syrup, salt, and water together, without stirring, to 250° on a candy thermometer or until a small amount dropped into cold water will form a firm ball. Pour the hot syrup slowly over stiffly beaten egg white, beating constantly. Add vanilla and continue beating until frosting is cool and thick enough to spread. Cut marshmallows into small pieces and mix into frosting. Spread frosting over top and sides of cooled Chocolate Nut Cake. *Makes enough for one 8-inch loaf.*

MENU

❦

Old South Fried Prairie Chicken

American Fried Potatoes

Buttermilk Biscuits (see page 7)

Farmstead Onions and Apples

Cucumbers in Sour Cream

Pineapple Basket

OLD SOUTH FRIED PRAIRIE CHICKEN

2 *3-pound prairie chickens, cut into serving pieces*
3 *cups all-purpose flour*
1 *teaspoon poultry seasoning*
2 *eggs*
⅓ *cup milk*
   Peanut oil for frying
   Salt and pepper to taste
1 *recipe Southern-Style Cream Gravy*

Preheat oven to 325°. Wash the chicken pieces, but do not dry them; just shake off excess water. Divide the flour into two equal mounds, adding the poultry seasoning to one mound. Beat the eggs lightly with the milk. Heat 1 inch oil in a large skillet over medium heat.

Dredge the chicken pieces in the seasoned flour, shaking off the excess, then in the egg mixture. Dredge in unseasoned flour.

131

Fry for about 15 minutes to a rich golden brown on both sides, turning once.

Transfer each piece as it is done to an ovenproof dish, taking care not to break the crusts. Bake at 325° for 45 to 60 minutes or until the chicken is cooked through. Season with salt and pepper before serving hot with Southern-Style Cream Gravy. *Serves 6.*

SOUTHERN-STYLE CREAM GRAVY

3 tablespoons flour
6 tablespoons pan drippings from chicken
1¾ cups heavy cream
  Salt and pepper to taste

Add flour to pan drippings and mix to a smooth paste. Stir in cream and bring to a boil over medium heat, stirring constantly. Scrape the bottom of the pan to loosen any brown bits. Season to taste. Serve hot. *Serves 6.*

AMERICAN FRIED POTATOES

6 large potatoes
1 clove garlic
3 tablespoons bacon fat
  Salt and pepper to taste
½ teaspoon minced onion

Peel potatoes and slice very thin. Rub skillet with the cut edge of a clove of garlic. Add fat and melt over medium heat. Add potatoes, salt, pepper, and onion. Sauté, turning occasionally so that potatoes brown evenly on all sides. Cook about 25 to 30 minutes or until tender and light brown. *Serves 6.*

FARMSTEAD ONIONS AND APPLES

¼ cup butter
2 cups sliced onions
3 cups peeled, cored, and quartered apples
  Salt and pepper to taste

132

Heat butter in a heavy skillet over medium heat. Add onions and apples. Cover and let steam 20 minutes, stirring occasionally, until apples are soft and onions tender and slightly browned. Season with salt and pepper to taste. Serve hot as a vegetable. *Serves 6.*

CUCUMBERS IN SOUR CREAM

3 *large cucumbers*
1 *cup thick sour cream*
1 *tablespoon chopped onion*
3 *tablespoons vinegar*
¼ *teaspoon salt*
⅛ *teaspoon white pepper*

Peel cucumbers. Run tines of fork lengthwise on the cucumber and cut crosswise into thin slices. Combine remaining ingredients and pour over sliced cucumber. Marinate 30 minutes before serving. *Serves 6.*

Chapter Three

WATERFOWL

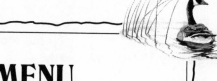

MENU
❧

Barbecued Duck

Pilgrim Succotash

Home Fries

Applesauce Cake

BARBECUED DUCK

2 5-pound ducks, cleaned and halved
1 clove garlic, crushed
¼ cup melted butter
¼ cup salad oil
¼ cup lemon juice
1 tablespoon grated onion
1 tablespoon paprika
⅓ cup catsup
⅛ teaspoon black pepper

Preheat oven to 400°. Place duck halves, split side down, on rack in a shallow baking pan. Rub with crushed garlic and brush with melted butter. Roast, uncovered, at 400° for 15 minutes. Combine remaining ingredients in a small saucepan and bring to a sim-

137

mer. Baste ducks with sauce and lower oven temperature to 350°. Continue roasting for 40 to 50 minutes or until ducks are tender, basting every 10 minutes. *Serves 4.*

PILGRIM SUCCOTASH

> 2 cups young lima beans, freshly shelled
> ½ cup light cream
> 2 cups fresh corn, cut from the cob
> 3 tablespoons sweet butter
>   Salt and pepper to taste

Simmer lima beans in just enough salted water to keep them from sticking. When the beans are almost tender, stir in the cream and corn. Cover and simmer until the corn is tender, but no more than 5 minutes. Stir in butter and season to taste with salt and pepper. Serve immediately. *Serves 4 to 6.*

HOME FRIES *nice*

> 1½ tablespoons bacon fat
> ¼ cup grated onion
> 5 medium cooked potatoes, cubed
>   Salt and pepper to taste
> 1 tablespoon chopped fresh parsley

Melt bacon fat in heavy iron skillet over medium heat. Add grated onion and sauté for 5 minutes. Add sliced cooked potatoes. Season with salt and pepper to taste. Raise heat and cook quickly to brown. When browned, remove to serving dish and sprinkle with chopped parsley. *Serves 4.*

APPLESAUCE CAKE

> 1¾ cups sifted cake flour
> 1 teaspoon baking soda
> ½ teaspoon salt
> 1½ teaspoons cinnamon

1 teaspoon allspice
1 teaspoon nutmeg
¼ teaspoon cloves
½ cup butter
1 cup sugar
1 egg, beaten
1 cup unsweetened applesauce
1 recipe Caramel Fudge Icing

Preheat oven to 350°. Sift flour, soda, salt, and spices together three times. Cream butter with sugar until fluffy. Add egg and beat thoroughly. Add sifted dry ingredients and applesauce alternately in small additions. Pour into a greased and floured 8-by-8-inch-square pan and bake, at 350°, for 45 to 60 minutes or until knife inserted in center of cake comes out clean. Remove from pan and cool on wire rack. Frost with Caramel Fudge Icing. *Serves 4 to 6.*

CARAMEL FUDGE ICING

2 cups brown sugar
1 cup granulated sugar
1 cup sour cream
1 tablespoon butter
1 teaspoon vanilla

Combine sugars and sour cream. Cook mixture, stirring constantly, to 238° on a candy thermometer or until a small amount forms a soft ball when dropped into cold water. Add butter and vanilla and cool to lukewarm without stirring. When cool, beat until thick enough to spread. If frosting becomes too thick while spreading, beat in a few drops of hot water. *Enough to frost two 9-inch layers.*

MENU
❧

Beaver Pond English Duckling

Wild Rice
with Snow Peas

Peach and Berry Salad

Baked Indian Pudding

BEAVER POND ENGLISH DUCKLING

2 5- to 6-pound ducklings
3 tablespoons melted butter
3 tablespoons chopped shallots
2 tablespoons green peppercorns
¼ cup brandy
1 cup white wine
1½ cups beef stock
  Salt to taste
2 teaspoons cornstarch
1 tablespoon cold water
2 tablespoons whipping cream

Preheat oven to 325°. Place ducks on rack in a large roasting pan. Roast at 325° for ½ hour per pound, or until fork-tender.

Remove from oven and keep warm. Melt butter in a saucepan over medium heat. Add shallots, 1 tablespoon peppercorns, brandy, wine, and pan drippings; bring to a boil. Continue cooking until reduced to about ¾ cup liquid. Add beef stock, remaining peppercorns, and salt; bring to a boil. Dissolve cornstarch in cold water and whisk into sauce. Boil to reduce sauce to 1 cup. Whisk in cream. Cut duck in half. Crisp skin under broiler. Remove from broiler and spoon peppercorn sauce over duck and serve. *Serves 4 to 6.*

WILD RICE WITH SNOW PEAS

1 cup wild rice
2 scallions
1 tablespoon butter
Salt to taste
2 cups or more chicken broth
¼ pound (1 cup) snow peas
4 large mushrooms
1 4-ounce can water chestnuts, drained
2 tablespoons peanut or salad oil
Salt and freshly ground black pepper to taste
¼ cup toasted almonds

Wash rice thoroughly, changing the water several times. Cut scallion stems diagonally into 2-inch lengths. Finely chop the white part of the scallions. Melt butter in a large saucepan. Add the white scallion and sauté until tender. Add the rice, salt, and 2 cups chicken broth. Bring to a boil, stir once, and reduce the heat. Cover tightly and cook over low heat until the rice is tender and the liquid is absorbed, about 35 minutes. If necessary, add more broth as the rice cooks.

Remove the ends and strings from the peas. Cut the mushrooms and water chestnuts into thin slices. Heat the oil in a large skillet over medium heat. Add the scallion stems, peas, mushrooms, and water chestnuts; sauté only until the mushrooms are tender.

Stir vegetables into rice; add salt and pepper to taste. Place in serving bowl and sprinkle with toasted almonds. Serve immediately. *Serves 4 to 6.*

PEACH AND BERRY SALAD

4 large fresh peaches
1 tablespoon fresh lemon juice
1 head butter lettuce, separated
3 dozen red raspberries
½ cup sour cream
1 tablespoon fresh lime juice
½ teaspoon honey
    Fresh cracked black pepper

Peel, pit, and slice peaches. Coat with lemon juice to keep from turning brown. Place equal amounts of sliced peaches on a bed of butter lettuce. Sprinkle with several fresh raspberries. Whisk together sour cream, lime juice, and honey. Drizzle over fruit and finish with a generous sprinkle of fresh cracked black pepper. *Serves 4 to 6.*

BAKED INDIAN PUDDING

1 cup yellow granulated cornmeal
½ cup black molasses
¼ cup granulated sugar
¼ cup butter
¼ teaspoon salt
¼ teaspoon baking soda
2 eggs
6 cups hot milk

Preheat oven to 450°. Mix the first seven ingredients thoroughly with 3 cups hot milk and bake at 450° for 30 minutes, or until mixture boils. Remove from heat and stir in remaining hot milk. Pour into a well-greased 2-quart casserole and bake, at 275°, for about 3 hours or until pudding is firm and light brown. Serve hot with heavy cream or ice cream. *Serves 4 to 8.*

MENU

❧

Duck and Beans

Orange and Onion Salad

Raisin Bread with Cream Cheese

Maple Nut Cake

DUCK AND BEANS

4 duck pieces, about ¾ pound each
  Salt and freshly ground black pepper to taste
1 onion, chopped
1 clove garlic, crushed
2 cups chicken broth
1 tablespoon sherry
1 15-ounce can baked beans in tomato sauce
1 tablespoon tomato catsup
⅓ pound spicy garlic sausage, chopped
1 teaspoon dried thyme
1 bay leaf
4 tablespoons chopped fresh parsley
1 cup fresh white bread crumbs

Preheat oven to 375°. Prick the duck pieces all over, using a fork. Season with salt and pepper and place on a rack in a roasting pan. Roast 1¼ hours at 375° or until duck pieces are cooked through and the juices run clear when the meat is pierced with a fine skewer. Remove and drain on paper towel. Place in a large casserole. Turn the oven down to 350°.

Drain off all but 1 tablespoon of fat from the roasting pan. Set over medium heat on the top of the stove. Add onion and garlic and sauté for 2 minutes.

Gradually stir in the broth and sherry. Bring to a boil, stirring constantly. Add baked beans, tomato catsup, garlic sausage, thyme, and bay leaf. Season to taste with salt and freshly ground black pepper. Pour over duck. Cover and bake at 350° for 30 minutes.

Increase oven temperature to 425°. Mix the parsley and bread crumbs together and sprinkle evenly over the surface of the casserole. Return to the oven and cook an additional 15 minutes, uncovered, to brown the topping. Remove from heat and serve immediately. *Serves 4.*

ORANGE AND ONION SALAD

2 large navel oranges, peeled and sectioned
2 medium red onions, peeled and thinly sliced
1 bunch watercress
4 tablespoons extra virgin olive oil
1 tablespoon fresh orange juice
1 teaspoon fresh cracked black pepper
½ teaspoon minced fresh rosemary

Toss all ingredients together to blend. Serve immediately. *Serves 4.*

RAISIN BREAD

3 cups cake flour
3 teaspoons baking powder
½ cup dark brown sugar
1 egg

¾ cup milk
⅛ cup melted butter
1½ cups dark raisins
½ cup finely chopped walnuts

Preheat oven to 350°. Sift together flour and baking powder. Blend in sugar. Stir egg, milk, and melted butter together and add to dry ingredients. Blend well. Stir in raisins and nuts. Pour into greased and floured 9-by-5-inch loaf pan. Bake at 350° for 1 hour or until well browned and toothpick inserted in center comes out clean. Slice and serve warm with cream cheese. *Makes 1 loaf.*

MAPLE NUT CAKE

½ cup vegetable shortening
4 tablespoons butter
¾ cup pure maple syrup
1½ teaspoons vanilla extract
3 eggs
2½ cups plus 2 tablespoons all-purpose flour
3¾ teaspoons baking powder
½ teaspoon salt
⅓ cup milk
½ cup chopped pecans
½ cup chopped walnuts
1 recipe Maple Frosting, or 1 recipe Maple Glaze

Preheat oven to 375°. Beat the shortening and butter together until light and fluffy. Cream in maple syrup, a bit at a time, blending after each addition until the syrup is completely absorbed. Add the vanilla extract. Beat the eggs until frothy. Add to batter and continue beating until well blended.

Sift the flour. Resift with the baking powder and salt. Add dry ingredients to batter alternately with the milk, stirring only long enough to moisten after each addition of flour. Mix in the chopped pecans and walnuts and pour the batter into two greased and floured 9-inch cake pans.

Bake at 375° for 25 to 30 minutes or until tops spring back at the touch of a fingertip. Remove from oven and let stand for 10 minutes before removing from pans. Cool on wire racks to room temperature before frosting with Maple Frosting or Maple Glaze. *Serves 6 to 10.*

MAPLE FROSTING

1½ cups maple syrup
3 egg whites
⅛ teaspoon salt
1½ teaspoons vanilla

Cook the syrup to 238° on candy thermometer, or until a small amount forms a soft ball when it is dropped in cold water. Remove from heat and cool slightly.

Beat the egg whites until they form stiff peaks, sprinkling in salt as you beat. Pour the maple syrup into the egg whites in a thin stream, beating constantly at high speed with an electric mixer until the syrup is well blended and the frosting holds a stiff peak. Beat in the vanilla and frost cake immediately. *Enough to frost two 9-inch cakes.*

MAPLE GLAZE

4 tablespoons butter
¼ cup heavy cream
1½ cups maple syrup

Place all ingredients in a saucepan and bring to a boil. Stir briefly and cook at full boil for 2 minutes. Cool slightly, then beat with a rotary beater until the glaze thickens, fluffs, and reaches spreading consistency. *Enough to glaze center and top of a two-layer, 9-inch cake.*

MENU

❦

Shiocton Duck
with Caraway Sour Cream Sauce

Mandarin Rice

Lemon-Buttered Brussels Sprouts

Key Lime Pie

SHIOCTON DUCK WITH CARAWAY SOUR CREAM SAUCE

     3 *2½-pound ducks, skinned and cut into serving pieces*
    ½ *cup butter*
     5 *tablespoons flour*
     4 *cups sour cream*
       Salt and pepper to taste
  1⅓ *tablespoons caraway seeds*
  1½ *pounds mushrooms, sliced*
    ¼ *cup minced chives*
     3 *tablespoons minced parsley*

Preheat oven to 325°. Rinse the duck pieces and pat dry. Melt the butter in a heavy skillet over medium heat. Brown the duck pieces on all sides. Transfer to a large baking dish.

147

Stir the flour into the butter remaining in the skillet, mixing until smooth. Add the sour cream and simmer for 3 or 4 minutes, stirring constantly. Stir in salt and pepper to taste, caraway seeds, mushrooms, and chives. Blend well and spoon the sauce over the duck. Cover and bake, at 325° for 30 minutes or until sauce is bubbly and thick and duck is well cooked. Remove from heat and place on warm serving platter with Mandarin Rice. *Serves 8.*

MANDARIN RICE

2 *tablespoons butter*
3 *tablespoons finely chopped celery*
3 *tablespoons finely chopped onion*
2 *cups bread cubes*
 Salt and pepper to taste
2½ *cups Mandarin or navel orange sections*
1 *teaspoon poultry seasoning*
1½ *cups cooked rice*

Preheat oven to 325°. Melt butter in heavy skillet over medium heat. Add celery and onion. Lower heat and sauté for about 10 minutes or until vegetables are limp. Blend together with remaining ingredients. Spoon into greased 1½-quart casserole. Cover and bake at 325° for about 30 minutes, or until top is well browned. Serve with Shiocton Duck. *Serves 8.*

LEMON-BUTTERED BRUSSELS SPROUTS

2 *baskets Brussels sprouts, trimmed and washed*
3 *tablespoons butter*
1 *tablespoon fresh lemon juice*
1 *tablespoon chopped fresh chives*
 Salt and pepper to taste

Cook Brussels sprouts in boiling salted water for about 15 minute, or until just tender. Drain well. Return to saucepan and add remaining ingredients. Stir to coat. Serve immediately. *Serves 8.*

KEY LIME PIE

1 tablespoon gelatin
¼ teaspoon salt
1 cup sugar
½ cup fresh lime juice
1 teaspoon finely grated lime rind
¼ cup water
4 eggs, separated
2 cups whipped cream
3 drops green food coloring
1 9-inch baked pie shell (see Plain Pastry, page 8)

In a small saucepan, combine gelatin, salt, ½ cup sugar, lime juice, rind, water, and egg yolks. Cook, stirring constantly, until mixture comes to a boil. Remove from heat and cool until it begins to set.

Beat egg whites until they are stiff, gradually adding the remaining ½ cup sugar. Fold in 1 cup whipped cream. Fold into the lime custard. Color slightly with food coloring. Pour into baked pie shell, top with the remaining cup whipped cream and refrigerate for at least 1 hour before serving. *Serves 6 to 8.*

MENU

Hudson Valley Duckling

Palisades Vegetables: Creamed Celery with Pecans

Yummy Yams

Company Rice Pudding

HUDSON VALLEY DUCKLING

    1 5-pound duck, quartered
  1/3 cup honey
 4½ teaspoons Cointreau
    1 teaspoon dry mustard
    6 orange slices
    4 maraschino cherries

Preheat broiler. Place duck in broiler pan. Combine honey, Cointreau, and dry mustard. Brush duckling with honey mixture. Broil until lightly brown. Remove from broiler and place on rack of roasting pan. Lower oven to 350° and bake for about 30 minutes or until well done. Baste and prick duck as it roasts. Garnish with orange slices and cherries. *Serves 4.*

PALISADES VEGETABLES:
CREAMED CELERY WITH PECANS

4 cups celery, cut diagonally in ½-inch pieces
4 tablespoons butter
2 tablespoons all-purpose flour
2 cups milk
  Salt and pepper to taste
¾ cup pecan halves
  Buttered bread crumbs

Preheat oven to 400°. Boil celery until tender in enough water to cover. Drain. Melt butter in small saucepan over medium heat. Stir in flour. Add milk, stirring until thick and smooth. Add salt and pepper and well-drained celery. Spoon into greased 1½-quart casserole. Top with pecans and cover with buttered bread crumbs. Bake at 400° for 15 minutes or until top is brown and bubbly. *Serves 4.*

YUMMY YAMS

2 large baked yams
¼ cup butter
1 tablespoon honey
1 tablespoon orange juice
½ teaspoon ground cinnamon
½ teaspoon dry mustard
1 tablespoon melted butter
2 tablespoons bread crumbs

Preheat oven to 350°. Split yams in half lengthwise. Scoop out pulp, being careful not to break skin.

Whip pulp with butter, honey, orange juice, cinnamon, and mustard. Stuff back into each half. Brush with melted butter and sprinkle with bread crumbs. Bake at 350° for 15 minutes or until top is bubbly. Serve immediately. *Serves 4.*

COMPANY RICE PUDDING

1 cup long-grain rice
2½ cups boiling water
1 recipe Vanilla Custard
2 cups peach preserves
4 tablespoons rum
  Whipped cream, optional

Add rice to boiling water. Cover and cook over low heat until rice is cooked but quite firm, about 20 minutes.

Fold cooked rice into Vanilla Custard. Spoon half into a glass serving bowl. Thin peach preserves with rum and spread half over the rice custard in bowl. Add the remaining custard and top with the remaining preserves. Refrigerate until well chilled (or overnight). Serve with whipped cream, if desired. *Serves 4 to 6.*

VANILLA CUSTARD

¾ cup granulated sugar
8 egg yolks
1¾ cups milk
1¼ cups heavy cream
½ vanilla bean, split

Place the sugar in the top half of a double boiler. Add the egg yolks, beating until mixture is thick and pale yellow. Combine the milk, cream, and vanilla bean in another saucepan. Bring to the scalding point.

Gradually add the hot milk mixture to the sugar and eggs, stirring constantly. Set over hot water and continue to stir until the custard thickens enough to coat the spoon. Do not allow the mixture to boil or it will curdle.

Remove the pan from the heat and strain the custard through a sieve. Cool, stirring from time to time. *Makes approximately 3 cups.*

MENU

Cherry Duck

Parsley Noodles

Caesar Salad

Popovers

Raisin Butterscotch Pie

CHERRY DUCK

2 *mallard ducks, cleaned and quartered*
2 *tablespoons butter*
2 *tablespoons sugar*
1 *tablespoon finely minced fresh ginger*
  Dash of salt
1 *tablespoon finely minced orange peel*
¼ *cup orange juice*
2 *1-pound cans pitted Bing cherries, drained (reserve syrup)*
2 *tablespoons cornstarch*
¼ *cup cherry-flavored brandy (or orange juice)*

Preheat oven to 350°. Wash ducks and pat dry with paper towel. Melt butter in a heavy skillet over medium heat. Brown duck on all sides. Place duck, skin-side up, in oblong baking dish. In a small saucepan, over medium heat, combine sugar, ginger, salt, orange

153

peel, orange juice, and ¾ cup reserved cherry syrup. Heat to boiling. Remove from heat and pour over duck. Bake, basting occasionally, at 350° for 45 to 60 minutes, or until duck juices are no longer pink when meat is pricked with fork and meat is no longer pink when cut between leg and body. Remove meat to warm platter and keep warm. In small saucepan, over high heat, combine remaining cherry syrup with cornstarch. Cook, stirring constantly, until mixture thickens and boils. Boil and stir 1 minute. Skim excess fat from pan juices. Add pan juices, cherries, and brandy to sauce. Heat through. Pour over ducks and serve immediately. *Serves 4 to 6.*

PARSLEY NOODLES

6 cups hot cooked egg noodles
4 tablespoons chopped fresh parsley
1 teaspoon poppy seeds
¼ cup melted butter
  Salt and pepper to taste

Mix all ingredients together. Serve immediately. *Serves 4 to 6.*

CAESAR SALAD

1 clove garlic
1 anchovy fillet
2 ounces olive oil
1 ounce red wine vinegar
¼ teaspoon dry mustard
¼ teaspoon Worcestershire sauce
1 head romaine lettuce, washed, dried, and torn into bite-size pieces
1 coddled egg
½ lemon
¼ cup grated Parmesan cheese

Rub garlic and anchovy into the sides of a wooden salad bowl. Add olive oil and red vinegar, dry mustard, and Worcestershire sauce; stir vigorously in the bottom of the bowl. Add romaine. Toss to coat. Break coddled egg over salad. Squeeze lemon over top.

Toss thoroughly, sprinkle Parmesan cheese on top, and serve immediately. *Serves 4 to 6.*

POPOVERS

    1 cup flour
    ¼ teaspoon salt
    2 tablespoons melted butter
    2 eggs
    1½ cups milk

Preheat oven to 450°. Using the steel blade, mix all ingredients together in a food processor. Generously butter muffin (or popover) pans. Place in preheated oven. When the pans are piping hot, remove from oven and fill each cup about one-third full. Return to oven and bake at 450° for 20 minutes. Reduce heat to 350° and bake for another 15 minutes. Do not open oven door until time elapses. Serve hot. *Makes approximately 1 dozen popovers.*

RAISIN BUTTERSCOTCH PIE

    3 tablespoons butter
    ¾ cup brown sugar
    2¼ cups milk
    1 tablespoon cornstarch
    1 cup raisins, ground
    ⅛ teaspoon salt
    2 egg yolks
    2 teaspoons vanilla
    1 9-inch baked pie shell (see Plain Pastry, page 8)
    1 recipe Brown Sugar Meringue

Preheat oven to 325°. In top half of double boiler, heat butter and sugar together. Stir in 2 cups milk and scald, stirring to dissolve sugar. Combine cornstarch, remaining milk, raisins, salt, and egg yolks and beat well. Add to milk mixture and cook over boiling water until thick, stirring constantly. Add vanilla. Pour into baked pie shell, top with Brown Sugar Meringue, and bake as directed.

BROWN SUGAR MERINGUE

2 egg whites
4 tablespoons brown sugar
½ teaspoon vanilla

Beat egg whites until frothy. Add sugar and vanilla gradually and beat until stiff. Pile on pie, making sure to seal edges. Bake at 325° for 15 to 18 minutes or until golden. Serve warm. *Serves 4 to 6.*

MENU

🦆

*Chesapeake Duck
with Pecan Stuffing*

*Winter Squash
with Cranberries*

Tangy Coleslaw

Fresh Pineapple Pie

CHESAPEAKE DUCK WITH PECAN STUFFING

2 2½-pound wild ducks, dressed and cleaned
4 cups soft bread crumbs
1 cup finely chopped celery
1 cup finely chopped onion
1 cup seedless raisins
1 cup chopped pecan meats
½ teaspoon salt
½ cup milk, scalded
2 eggs, beaten
6 slices bacon or salt pork
1 cup tomato catsup
¼ cup Worcestershire sauce
¼ cup A-1 sauce
½ cup chili sauce
5 full sprigs fresh parsley, optional
6 orange slices, optional
¼ cup candied cranberries, optional

157

Preheat oven to 350°. Mix bread crumbs, celery, onions, raisins, nuts, and salt together. Add hot milk to the beaten eggs and add to dry mixture. Fill ducks with stuffing. Close with poultry pins or by sewing. Place in roaster and cover each duck with 3 strips of bacon. Roast, uncovered, at 350°, allowing 15 to 20 minutes per pound. Twenty minutes before serving time, combine the next four ingredients and baste the ducks. Garnish with optional parsley, orange slices, and candied cranberries. Skim fat from sauce and serve with ducks. *Serves 4.*

WINTER SQUASH WITH CRANBERRIES

4 *cups cooked, mashed winter squash*
2 *eggs, beaten*
⅓ *cup melted butter*
¼ *cup granulated sugar*
1½ *cups raw cranberries or lingonberries (halved if they are large)*
Salt and pepper to taste
Ground nutmeg

Preheat oven to 400°. Whip squash with eggs and 3 tablespoons butter. Stir in sugar, cranberries, salt, and pepper. Spoon into greased 2-quart casserole, top with remaining butter, and sprinkle with nutmeg. Bake, uncovered, 30 to 40 minutes or until bubbly. *Serves 4 to 8.*

TANGY COLESLAW

4 *cups shredded cabbage*
½ *cup sour cream*
½ *cup mayonnaise*
1 *tablespoon Dijon mustard*
½ *teaspoon celery seeds*
1 *tablespoon vinegar*
1 *teaspoon fresh lemon juice*
2 *teaspoons sugar*
2 *tablespoons chopped capers*

Mix all ingredients together. Cover and let stand at least 30 minutes before serving. *Serves 4 to 6.*

FRESH PINEAPPLE PIE

2 *eggs*
1⅓ *cups sugar*
1 *tablespoon fresh lemon juice*
2 *cups shredded fresh pineapple*
1 *9-inch unbaked pie shell with lid (see Plain Pastry, page 8)*
1 *tablespoon butter*

Preheat oven to 450°. Beat eggs slightly. Add sugar, lemon juice, and pineapple. Pour filling into pie shell. Dot with butter and cover with top crust. Bake at 450° for 10 minutes. Reduce oven temperature to 350° and bake for 35 minutes longer or until pineapple is tender and crust is light brown. Serve warm with vanilla ice cream. *Serves 4 to 8.*

MENU

❧

Wild Duck in Peach Marinade

Wild Rice and Almonds

Sautéed Scallions

Chicory and Artichoke Salad

Old South Carrot Cake

WILD DUCK IN PEACH MARINADE

2 3-pound mallards, halved
1 16-to-20 ounce can peach slices
½ cup soy sauce
1 1-inch piece of fresh ginger, peeled and sliced
1 tablespoon butter
1 3-ounce package fresh mushrooms, quartered

Drain peaches, saving juice. Add half the peach slices to the reserved juice. Mix together the peaches, juice, soy sauce, and ginger. Pour over duck and marinate overnight.

Preheat oven to 350°. Remove ducks from marinade and wipe off excess sauce. Melt butter in a heavy skillet over medium heat and brown duck on both sides. When brown, place in shallow baking dish. Pour on marinade. Add mushrooms. Bake, covered, approximately 2 hours at 350° or until tender. Add water, if necessary. *Serves 4.*

WILD RICE AND ALMONDS

1 cup wild rice
4 cups cold water
1½ teaspoons salt
4 tablespoons butter
½ cup chopped shallots
10 medium mushrooms, chopped
1 large onion, chopped
Liver from duck, chopped
1 teaspoon poultry seasoning
1 cup coarsely chopped toasted almonds

Preheat oven to 350°. Wash rice in several changes of cold water. Cover with 4 cups cold water. Stir in 1 teaspoon salt and bring to a boil. Boil, uncovered, for 35 to 40 minutes or until tender. Drain and dry out over very low heat for 5 minutes.

Melt butter in heavy skillet over medium heat. Sauté the shallots, mushrooms, onion, liver, seasoning, and remaining ½ teaspoon salt until the onion is transparent. Stir in the nuts and rice. Bake at 350°, covered, for 30 minutes. Serve hot. *Serves 4.*

NOTE: This may also be used to stuff duck, goose, or other birds.

SAUTÉED SCALLIONS

4 bunches scallions
3 tablespoons butter
1 teaspoon brown sugar
½ teaspoon fresh lemon juice
Salt and pepper to taste

Wash and trim scallions. Melt butter in heavy skillet over medium heat. Add sugar and lemon juice. Stir to blend. Add scallions, salt, and pepper to taste. Lower heat and sauté for about 10 minutes, gently turning once to allow even cooking. Do not overcook. Scallions should be just tender. Serve immediately. *Serves 4.*

CHICORY AND ARTICHOKE SALAD

1 medium head chicory, washed, trimmed, and dried
1 cup sliced marinated artichoke hearts
1 cup fresh, toasted herb croutons
4 tablespoons green peppercorn mustard
½ cup virgin olive oil
1 tablespoon fresh lemon juice
  Salt and pepper to taste

Chop chicory into bite-size pieces. Mix together with artichokes and croutons. Whisk the mustard, oil, lemon juice, salt, and pepper together. Pour over salad and toss to coat. *Serves 4.*

OLD SOUTH CARROT CAKE

2 cups all-purpose flour
2 cups sugar
1 teaspoon baking powder
¼ teaspoon baking soda
1 teaspoon ground cinnamon
4 eggs
1 cup vegetable oil
2 cups grated carrots
1 recipe Deluxe Cream Cheese Frosting

Preheat oven to 375°. Combine dry ingredients and stir gently. Set aside. Combine eggs and oil, beating well. Fold in dry ingredients and carrots.

Spoon batter into three greased and floured 9-inch cake pans; bake at 375° for 25 minutes, or until cake tests done. Cake layers will be thin. Cool 10 minutes in pans. Remove from pans and cool on wire racks. Spread Deluxe Cream Cheese Frosting between layers and on top and sides of cake. *Serves 8.*

DELUXE CREAM CHEESE FROSTING

½ cup butter or margarine, softened
1 8-ounce package cream cheese, softened
2 cups confectioners' sugar
2 teaspoons vanilla extract
1 cup chopped pecans
1 cup flaked coconut

Combine butter and cream cheese. Beat until light and fluffy. Add sugar and vanilla, mixing well. Stir in pecans and coconut. *Makes enough for one three-layer cake.*

OTHER RECIPES

❧

CHARCOAL GRILLED DUCK BREASTS

4 duck breast fillets
4 bacon strips
  Salt and pepper to taste
2 beef bouillon cubes
1 cup water
1 tablespoon red currant jelly
½ teaspoon dry mustard
1 tablespoon sherry
1 tablespoon brandy
  Pinch of dried ground marjoram
  Pinch of dried ground oregano
  Grated rind of 1 orange

Prepare coals for grilling. Wrap each duck breast fillet with bacon. Fasten with toothpick. Season with salt and pepper. Charcoal broil over hot coals for exactly 2 minutes per side. Dissolve bouillon cubes in 1 cup water in chafing dish or electric skillet. Blend in jelly, mustard, sherry, brandy, and herbs. Simmer until slightly thick. Stir in orange rind. Place charcoal-broiled fillets in chafing dish. Cook for 5 minutes or until medium rare, basting constantly. *Serves 4.*

REMINGTON DUCK HASH

2 cups chopped cooked duck
¼ cup butter or margarine
1 small onion, chopped
2 cups diced cooked potatoes
½ cup chopped water chestnuts
½ cup diced green pepper
½ cup chicken broth
  Salt and pepper to taste
½ teaspoon grated lemon rind
¼ cup heavy cream
½ cup buttered soft bread crumbs

164

Preheat oven to 350°. Melt butter in a heavy skillet over medium heat. Add onion and cook until golden. Add potatoes and brown lightly. Stir in duck, water chestnuts, green pepper, broth, salt, pepper, lemon rind, and cream. Pack into greased shallow baking dish and sprinkle with crumbs. Bake at 350° for 30 minutes or until brown. Remove from oven and serve immediately. *Serves 4.*

NAPA VALLEY DUCKLING ROSÉ

1 5-pound duckling, quartered
Salt to taste
1 teaspoon paprika
1 teaspoon powdered ginger
1 tablespoon grated onion
1 cup rosé wine
⅓ cup brown sugar, firmly packed
⅓ cup granulated sugar
1 tablespoon cornstarch
1 teaspoon grated orange rind

Preheat oven to 400°. Remove excess fat from duckling and place in shallow baking pan. Roast, uncovered, at 400° for 30 minutes. Remove from oven and drain off fat. Sprinkle with salt, paprika, ginger, and onion. Pour ¼ cup wine into pan. Cover tightly with foil and continue roasting 45 minutes longer or until tender. Mix remaining wine and other ingredients in saucepan over medium heat. Cook, stirring constantly, until thick. Pour over duckling and roast, uncovered, for about 10 minutes longer or until glazed; baste frequently. *Serves 4.*

DUCK SALAD WITH TARRAGON HONEY SAUCE

1 4½-pound duck
  Salt to taste
2 tablespoons clear honey
2 tablespoons hot water
2 heads endive, separated
1 bunch watercress, divided into small sprigs
2 oranges, divided into segments
4 tablespoons vegetable oil
1 tablespoon tarragon vinegar
1 tablespoon fresh orange juice
  Pinch of sugar
½ teaspoon Dijon-style mustard
  Salt and freshly ground black pepper to taste

Preheat oven to 350°. Pat the duck dry inside and out with paper towels. Prick the skin all over with a fork and sprinkle with salt, to taste.

Place the duck, breast-side up, on a rack in a roasting pan. Roast at 350° for 1 hour. Drain fat from pan. Blend honey and hot water and brush the duck all over. Return duck to the oven and roast an additional hour (for well-done duck), basting two to three times to glaze and brown. Drain the duck over the pan, transfer to a plate and let sit until completely cold, for 3 to 4 hours.

When cold, divide the duck into 4 pieces and place on serving dishes. Garnish each with equal portions of endive leaves, watercress sprigs, and orange segments.

Whisk remaining ingredients together. Pour over the duck salad just before serving. *Serves 4.*

BARBECUED BLUEBILL

2 bluebills, cleaned and halved
1 clove garlic, crushed
¼ cup melted butter or margarine
¼ cup salad oil
¼ cup lemon juice
1 tablespoon grated onion

166

1 tablespoon paprika
⅓ cup catsup
⅛ teaspoon black pepper

Preheat oven to 400°. Place duck halves, split side down, in a shallow baking pan. Rub with crushed garlic and brush with melted butter or margarine. Roast, uncovered, at 400° for 10 to 15 minutes. Meanwhile, combine other ingredients and heat to simmering. Reduce oven temperature to 350° and baste with the sauce every 10 minutes until ducks are tender, 40 to 50 minutes. *Serves 4 to 6.*

MISSOURI FLATS MALLARD

2 mallards, cut into serving pieces
1 teaspoon salt
¼ teaspoon pepper
1 cup flour
⅓ cup butter or margarine
½ cup chopped onion
¼ cup chopped celery
½ cup water, chicken broth or light cream

Season duck pieces with salt and pepper and roll in flour. Melt butter or margarine in a heavy skillet over medium heat and fry duck slowly for about 30 minutes or until brown on both sides. Turn only once. Remove duck pieces and sauté onion and celery in the pan drippings for 10 minutes. Return duck to pan, add liquid, and cover pan tightly. Simmer, over low heat, for 1 hour or until tender. *Serves 4.*

W. J.'s DUCK McGLUCK

  4 *duck breasts*
    Salt and pepper to taste
  1 *egg, beaten*
1½ *cups finely crushed cracker crumbs*
  ½ *cup melted butter*
  ½ *cup peanut oil*
  3 *tablespoons white wine*
  4 *cups hot cooked noodles*
  6 *tablespoons butter*
  1 *10-ounce can chicken broth*
  1 *10-ounce can cream of mushroom soup*
  ½ *pound mushrooms*
    Dash of garlic powder

Preheat oven to 350°. Cut each breast into 6 pieces, splitting if necessary so pieces are not too thick. Season with salt and pepper to taste. Dip in beaten egg and then 1 cup cracker crumbs. Heat butter and peanut oil together in a heavy skillet over medium heat. Add duck pieces and fry until golden brown on all sides. Add 1 tablespoon white wine and cook for 3 minutes.

Mix noodles with 2 tablespoons of butter. Set aside. Mix the undiluted broth and soup together. Set aside. Sauté the mushrooms in 2 tablespoons butter and 2 tablespoons white wine for 10 minutes. Add to soup.

Butter a 2-quart casserole and place half the noodles in it. Cover with duck pieces. Pour over half the soup. Top with remaining noodles and pour on remaining soup. Sprinkle with remaining crumbs and dash of garlic powder. Dot with remaining butter (add a couple more dashes of wine if you wish), cover and bake at 350° for 20 minutes. Uncover and bake 10 or 15 minutes more until bubbly and golden on top. *Serves 4.*

CHEESE-STUFFED BLUEBILL BREASTS

  3 *whole bluebill duck breasts, split in half*
 10 *ounces chopped spinach*
1½ *cups shredded Gouda cheese*

½ *cup fresh bread crumbs*
½ *cup shredded carrots*
½ *cup sliced green onion*
¼ *cup plus 2 tablespoons chopped parsley*
  2 *tablespoons snipped fresh dill*
    Salt and pepper to taste
  1 *egg, well beaten*
¼ *cup butter*
  2 *tablespoons lemon juice*

Preheat oven to 375°. Combine spinach, cheese, crumbs, carrots, onion, ¼ cup parsley, dill, salt, pepper, and egg. When well blended, stuff duck breasts by spooning between breast meat and skin. Place, skin side up, in shallow baking dish. Combine butter, lemon juice, and remaining parsley. Spread over duck. Bake at 375° for 45 minutes or until tender. Baste frequently with pan drippings. *Serves 6.*

MENU

❧

*Canada Goose
with Sweet Brandy Sauce*

Creamed Potatoes in Shells

Cauliflower and Mushroom Salad

Bordeaux Apples

CANADA GOOSE WITH SWEET BRANDY SAUCE

1 6-pound goose
 Salt to taste
1 large onion, peeled
2 apples, cored and quartered
1 medium potato, halved
6 to 8 strips bacon
1 recipe Sweet Brandy Sauce

Preheat oven to 300°. Rub cavity generously with salt. Place onion, apple quarters and potato halves inside goose. Cover goose with strips of smoked bacon. Place in 300° oven and bake for approximately 3 hours or at 30 minutes per pound of goose. Baste every 15 minutes of last hour with Sweet Brandy Sauce. Serve with warm Sweet Brandy Sauce. *Serves 6.*

170

SWEET BRANDY SAUCE

¾ *cup honey*
½ *cup brown sugar*
½ *cup red Chianti wine*
½ *teaspoon Worcestershire sauce*
 2 *ounces brandy*

Mix all ingredients in a small saucepan over medium heat. Stir briskly for 2 minutes, or until sugar is dissolved. Serve warm. *Makes 1¾ cups.* (Mrs. Joe Bartolo, Burlington, Wisconsin)

CREAMED POTATOES IN SHELLS

6 *medium potatoes*
1 *tablespoon melted butter*
1 *teaspoon salt*
2 *tablespoons diced pimiento*
2 *cups thin White Sauce (see page 76)*
2 *tablespoons grated cheddar cheese*
  Paprika

Preheat oven to 400°. Scrub potatoes well. Dry and rub with butter. Bake at 400° for 1 hour or until tender. Cut a lengthwise slice from top of each potato and, with a small spatula, carve out the pulp in small cubes and remove carefully, keeping the shells intact. Sprinkle with salt. Add potato cubes and pimiento to white sauce. Mix lightly and refill potato shells. Sprinkle with cheese and paprika. Return to oven to reheat and melt cheese. *Serves 6.*

CAULIFLOWER AND MUSHROOM SALAD

1 fresh cauliflower
Vinegar
½ pound fresh mushrooms, sliced thick
3 green onions, sliced thin
1 tablespoon diced pimiento
1 tablespoon chopped fresh parsley
1 cup Chef's Special Dressing
1 head Boston lettuce

Cut cauliflower in small rosettes; blanch 1 minute in boiling water with touch of vinegar. Cool. Combine with everything but Boston lettuce. Marinate 1 hour. Drain and reserve the dressing. Serve salad on a bed of Boston lettuce. Pour additional dressing on just before serving. *Serves 6.*

CHEF'S SPECIAL DRESSING

⅓ cup cider vinegar
½ teaspoon salt
1 teaspoon dry mustard
2 teaspoons sugar
½ teaspoon pepper
2 cloves garlic, crushed
Juice of 1 lemon
2 cups vegetable oil

Combine all ingredients, except vegetable oil. Allow to stand 10 minutes. Add oil. Shake well. *Makes 2½ cups.* (The Briar Inn, Jackson Point, Ontario, Canada)

BORDEAUX APPLES

6 tart cooking apples
Juice of ½ lemon
2 cups sugar
½ stick cinnamon, slivered
2 cups dry red wine (Bordeaux)

172

Preheat oven to 250°. Peel and core apples; place in cold water with lemon juice to prevent discoloring. Drain and put into oven-proof casserole with lid. Fill apple cavities with sugar and pour remaining sugar over them. Sprinkle with slivered cinnamon. Pour wine around apples. Cover and bake, at 250°, for 2 hours. Serve warm or chilled, with or without cream. *Serves 6.*

SHARON ANDERSON

MENU

Bagged Goose with Apples

Asparagus Soufflé

Stuffed Tomato Crowns

Ground Nut Cake
with Orange-Pecan Filling

BAGGED GOOSE WITH APPLES

1 6-pound wild goose
1 tablespoon flour
1 cup apple juice
½ cup chopped apple
½ cup chopped onion
  Salt and pepper to taste
1 teaspoon ground sage or 2 teaspoons chopped fresh sage
1 apple, quartered
1 onion, peeled and quartered
1 tablespoon butter, softened
1 teaspoon celery seed
⅓ cup red currant jelly
  Flour

Preheat oven to 325°. Shake flour in large (14-by-20-inch) oven cooking bag and place in a roasting pan. Add apple juice, apple, and onion to bag and turn to mix. Sprinkle goose cavity with salt, pepper and sage. Add apple and onion quarters. Close cavity with skewers and tie legs together. Spread butter over breast. Sprinkle with salt, pepper, and celery seed. Spread jelly over breast. Carefully place goose in bag. Close bag with nylon tie and make six ½-inch slits in top. Bake at 325° for 2½ hours or until tender. When done, remove goose and skim fat from broth in bag. Pour broth into a small saucepan. Whisk in 2 tablespoons flour for each cup of broth. Bring to a boil, stirring constantly, until thick. Serve over goose. *Serves 6.*

ASPARAGUS SOUFFLÉ

3 tablespoons butter, melted
3 tablespoons flour
1 cup milk
4 eggs, separated
2½ cups diced, cooked asparagus
   Salt and pepper to taste

Preheat oven to 325°. In a small saucepan, over medium heat, blend butter and flour. Gradually add milk. Lower heat and cook slowly, stirring constantly, until thick. Beat egg yolks until thick and lemon colored and whisk into sauce. Stir in asparagus, salt, and pepper. Beat egg whites until stiff. Fold into asparagus sauce and pour into greased 1½-quart casserole. Set in pan of hot water. Bake at 325° for about 45 minutes or until puffed and brown. Serve immediately. *Serves 6.*

STUFFED TOMATO CROWNS

6 firm tomatoes
2 tablespoons butter
2 teaspoons minced onion
½ teaspoon salt
⅛ teaspoon pepper
1½ cups soft bread crumbs
1 egg, lightly beaten
2 tablespoons chopped green pepper
2 tablespoons chopped celery
¼ cup finely chopped cabbage

Preheat oven to 375°. Wash tomatoes. Cut off tops and reserve. Scoop out pulp and chop. Melt butter in a small skillet over medium heat. Add onions and sauté until tender. Combine with remaining ingredients. Fill tomato shells. Replace tops and place in greased baking dish. Bake at 375° for about 30 minutes or until tomatoes are barely done. *Serves 6.*

GROUND NUT CAKE WITH ORANGE-PECAN FILLING

1 cup ground walnuts
¾ cup ground pecans
½ cup ground blanched almonds
2⅛ cups confectioners' sugar
2½ tablespoons cornstarch
9 egg whites
1 recipe Orange-Pecan Filling
12 walnut halves
1 egg white

Preheat oven to 275°. Combine the nuts and mix thoroughly with 2 cups sugar and the cornstarch. Beat the egg whites until they form stiff peaks. Gently fold the dry ingredients into the egg whites.

Butter and flour two 9-inch cake pans. Divide the batter equally between them and place in preheated oven. Bake at 275° for 1½ to 1¾ hours or until the cakes begin to pull away from the sides of the pans. Cool for 5 minutes in the pans. Remove and place on wire racks. Bring to room temperature. Spread the Orange-Pecan Filling over 1 cake layer. Carefully place the second layer on top of the filling. Use the ½ cup of filling thinned with the orange juice to frost the top of the cake. Dip the walnut halves in egg white, then in remaining ⅛ cup confectioners' sugar, and arrange attractively around the top. *Serves 12.*

ORANGE-PECAN FILLING

1½ *cups confectioners' sugar*
1½ *cups butter, softened*
  5 *tablespoons fresh orange juice*
⅛ *teaspoon orange extract*
1½ *cups ground pecans*

Cream sugar and butter until light and fluffy. Stir in 3 tablespoons orange juice and orange extract. Blend thoroughly. Set aside ½ cup of the filling. Stir ground pecans into the larger portion. Mix the reserved ½ cup of the filling with remaining 2 tablespoons of orange juice. Set aside. *Use to fill and glaze one ground nut cake.*

OTHER RECIPES

❦

Roast Goose with Potato Stuffing

1 8- to 10-pound goose
3 medium potatoes
4 tablespoons butter
2 onions, chopped
½ to ¾ cup heavy cream
   Salt and pepper to taste
3 tablespoons ice water
2 tablespoons flour
1½ cups chicken or goose broth

Preheat oven to 325°. Peel, quarter, and boil the potatoes until tender. Melt butter in a skillet over medium heat and sauté the onions until soft. Mash the potatoes with enough cream to make fluffy. Add the onions and salt and pepper to taste. Stuff potatoes into the cavity of the goose. Sew up or skewer closed. Rub the outside of the goose with more salt and pepper and prick the skin all over to release the fat as it melts during roasting.

Place the goose on a rack in a shallow roasting pan and roast at 325° for 30 minutes per pound. Pour off fat every 20 minutes. Spoon 3 tablespoons ice water over the goose during the last 15 minutes of roasting to crisp the skin.

Remove goose from oven. Skim fat from pan. Stir 2 tablespoons flour into remaining pan drippings. Add broth and cook, stirring constantly, until thick. Serve gravy with goose and potatoes. *Serves 4 to 6.*

Chapter Four

VENISON

MENU

❦

*Venison Steak
with Roquefort*

Rich Creamed Mushrooms

Camp Buckwheat Groats

Corn Relish

Autumn Fruit Salad Bowl

Betty's Blackberry Pie

VENISON STEAK WITH ROQUEFORT

1 2-pound venison steak, cut 1½ inches thick
¼ cup butter
¼ cup Roquefort cheese
Salt and pepper to taste

Cream together the butter and cheese. Add salt and pepper to taste. Trim excess fat from steak. Slash fat edge to prevent curling. Place steak on grill rack 6 inches above hot coals. Grill 10 to 15 minutes; turn. Spread top with cheese mixture and grill 15 minutes longer for medium steak. *Serves 4.*

RICH CREAMED MUSHROOMS

5 *tablespoons butter*
1 *pound mushrooms, trimmed and sliced*
Salt and pepper to taste
2 *tablespoons flour*
1½ *cups milk*

Melt butter in heavy skillet over medium heat. Add mushrooms and sauté for 15 minutes or until nearly tender. Stir in salt, pepper, and flour; mix well. Add milk gradually and simmer, stirring constantly, for 5 minutes or until thick and well blended. *Serves 4 to 6.*

CAMP BUCKWHEAT GROATS

2 *tablespoons butter*
¾ *cup chopped onion*
1 *tablespoon chopped fresh parsley*
1 *cup fine buckwheat groats*
1 *egg*
Salt and pepper to taste
2 *cups boiling chicken broth (or boiling water)*

Preheat oven to 375°. Melt butter in small skillet over medium heat. Add onion and parsley. Sauté for about 10 minutes or until onion is soft.

Mix the groats and egg together. Stir in onions and parsley, and salt and pepper to taste. Place in greased 1½-quart casserole. Pour in broth. Cover and bake at 375° for 20 minutes or until tender. *Serves 4 to 6.*

CORN RELISH

2 *cups whole kernel corn*
½ *cup finely chopped fresh green peppers*
½ *cup finely chopped fresh red peppers*
½ *cup finely chopped scallion*
1 *teaspoon mustard seed*

1 cup cider vinegar
1 teaspoon Dijon mustard
1 tablespoon sugar

Mix all ingredients. Cover and refrigerate for at least 24 hours before serving. Will keep refrigerated for 7 to 10 days. *Serves 4 to 12.*

AUTUMN FRUIT SALAD BOWL

1 head romaine, washed and pulled apart
½ medium pineapple, pared, cored, and sliced
1 grapefruit, peeled and sectioned
1 red apple, sliced
1 cup seedless red grapes
1 orange, peeled and sectioned
1 recipe Whipped Cream Mayonnaise

Line salad bowl with romaine. Place fruit on top of romaine in separate sections. Fill center with Whipped Cream Mayonnaise. *Serves 4.*

WHIPPED CREAM MAYONNAISE

½ cup mayonnaise
½ cup whipped cream
½ teaspoon grated fresh orange rind
   Dash of curry powder

Fold all ingredients together. Serve immediately. *Makes 1½ cups.*

BETTY'S BLACKBERRY PIE

4 cups blackberries, washed and well drained
4 tablespoons flour
1¼ cups granulated sugar
½ teaspoon grated orange rind
1 9-inch unbaked pie shell with lid (see Plain Pastry, page 8)

Preheat oven to 425°. Place the drained berries in a bowl and sift the flour and sugar over them. Add the orange rind and toss the berries gently. Pour into pastry-lined pie plate. Cover with top crust. Seal, prick, and bake at 425° for 15 minutes. Lower heat to 375° and bake for 30 minutes or until pastry is set and light brown. *Serves 4 to 8.*

MENU

*Venison
with Stilton and Walnuts*

Mashed Potatoes and Turnips

Sautéed Cherry Tomatoes

Pumpkin Hollow Pie

VENISON WITH STILTON AND WALNUTS

1 *3- to 3½-pound boned shoulder of venison*
¼ *pound Stilton cheese*
½ *cup chopped walnuts*
3 *tablespoons chopped fresh parsley and thyme*
1 *package stuffing mix*
   Salt and pepper to taste
1 *egg*
2 *tablespoons water*
1 *tablespoon vegetable oil*
1 *tablespoon butter*
2 *cups chicken broth*
1 *bouquet garni*
⅓ *pound mushrooms, sliced*
2 *teaspoons cornstarch*
2 *teaspoons water*
12 *toasted walnut halves, for garnish*

Preheat oven to 350°. Make the stuffing: Mash Stilton with a fork. Stir in the walnuts, herbs, and stuffing mix. Season with salt and pepper. Beat the egg into the water and stir into the stuffing.

Lay the venison skin side down on a board or work surface. Spread the stuffing mixture over it. Roll the venison up from one short end, then tie securely with string in several places to make a roll.

Heat the oil and butter in a large flameproof lidded casserole over medium heat. Add the venison. Raise heat and brown the meat on all sides. Drain excess fat from the casserole and pour in broth. Add bouquet garni. Cover with foil, then with the casserole top, and bake at 350° for 1 hour.

Remove from oven and add mushrooms. Cover as before and cook 30 minutes or until venison is cooked through and juices run clear when the meat is pierced with a skewer.

Place the venison on a warmed serving dish and remove the string. Set aside and keep warm. Place the casserole over medium heat and bring liquid to a boil. Blend the cornstarch and water in a small bowl, and stir in 2 tablespoons hot broth; mix into the casserole. Cook, stirring, 1 to 2 minutes until thick. Taste and adjust seasoning.

Carve venison into neat slices and coat with sauce. Garnish with walnuts. Pass remaining sauce in a warmed gravy boat. *Serves 4 to 6.*

MASHED POTATOES AND TURNIPS

2 *cups cooked potatoes*
2 *cups cooked white turnips*
3 *tablespoons butter*
½ *cup heavy cream*
   Salt and pepper to taste
2 *tablespoons melted butter*
¼ *tablespoon minced fresh parsley*

Preheat oven to 350°. Whip together the potatoes, turnips, butter, and heavy cream. Add salt and pepper to taste.

Pour into greased 1½-quart casserole. Pour melted butter on top. Sprinkle with parsley. Bake at 350° for 15 minutes. Serve immediately. *Serves 4 to 6.*

Sautéed Cherry Tomatoes

1 tablespoon butter
2 tablespoons olive oil
1 teaspoon minced fresh garlic
3 cups cherry tomatoes, washed and stemmed
  Salt and pepper to taste

Melt butter with olive oil in a heavy skillet over medium heat. Add garlic and cherry tomatoes. Lower heat and sauté for about 10 minutes or just until skin starts to pop. Salt and pepper to taste. Serve immediately. *Serves 4 to 6.*

Pumpkin Hollow Pie

1½ cups cooked pumpkin, whipped
¾ cup sugar
1½ cups half-and-half
 3 egg yolks
½ teaspoon ground cinnamon
½ teaspoon grated nutmeg
¼ teaspoon ground ginger
   Dash of salt
 3 egg whites, stiffly beaten
 1 9-inch unbaked pie shell (see Plain Pastry, page 8)
   Bourbon
   Whipped cream

Preheat oven to 350°. Combine pumpkin, sugar, half-and-half, egg yolks, spices and salt. Fold in beaten egg whites. Pour into pie shell. Bake at 350° for 45 minutes or until set. Remove from heat and cool slightly. When ready to serve, slice into serving portions. Poke a few knife slits into each slice and pour one scant teaspoon of bourbon on top. Top with a dollop of whipped cream. *Serves 4 to 8.*

MENU

✿

*Sour Mash Venison
Stroganoff Tennessee Style*

Buttered Noodles

*Zucchini and Carrots
with Fresh Mint*

Walnut Grove Salad

Blackberry Delight

SOUR MASH VENISON STROGANOFF TENNESSEE STYLE

   1 1½-pound venison steak, cut into ½-inch cubes
½ cup vegetable shortening
¾ cup flour
   1 6-ounce can sliced mushrooms
   1 small onion, minced
   1 clove garlic, minced
   1 10¾-ounce can condensed tomato soup, undiluted
   6 drops Tabasco sauce
   1 tablespoon Wild Turkey whiskey
   1 tablespoon Worcestershire sauce
   1 tablespoon A-1 Sauce
1½ cups commercial sour cream

Melt shortening in heavy skillet over medium heat. Dredge meat in flour and brown on all sides. Drain mushrooms; reserve liquid. Add mushrooms, onion, and garlic to meat. Combine soup with mushroom liquid, Tabasco, whiskey, Worcestershire sauce, and A-1 Sauce; pour over meat. Cover and simmer 1 hour or until tender. Just before serving, stir in sour cream. Heat, but do not boil. Serve over buttered noodles. *Serves 4.*

ZUCCHINI AND CARROTS WITH FRESH MINT

3 tablespoons butter
4 carrots, peeled and cut into ¼-inch slices
   Salt and freshly ground pepper to taste
4 zucchini (each about 8 inches long) cut in half lengthwise, then
   cut into ¼-inch slices
3 tablespoons chopped fresh mint leaves

Heat the butter to sizzling over medium heat in sauté pan. Lower heat and add carrots and salt and pepper to taste. Cover and cook for 5 minutes over low heat. Add zucchini, cover and cook at the same temperature 10 minutes more. Remove from heat. Sprinkle with mint leaves and serve. *Serves 4.*

WALNUT GROVE SALAD

½ pound cream cheese
¼ cup mayonnaise
3 tablespoons finely chopped walnuts
3 tablespoons finely chopped black olives
   Salt to taste
8 tomato slices, cut ¼ inch thick
1 green pepper, seeded and cut into strips
2 cups mix of torn salad greens
8 pitted black olives
8 4-inch celery sticks

Beat cheese and mayonnaise until smooth. Add nuts, chopped olives, and salt to taste. When blended, spread thickly on 4 tomato slices. Arrange pepper strips diagonally across filling and top each tomato with another slice; place on nest of greens. Place an olive on one end of each celery stick and cross two on each salad. *Serves 4.*

BLACKBERRY DELIGHT

1 cup flour
1½ teaspoons baking powder
¼ teaspoon salt
2 tablespoons sugar
½ cup milk
2 tablespoons melted butter
1 quart blackberries
2 cups sugar (approximately) (1) or less,
½ cup water
2 tablespoons butter

Mix together flour, baking powder, salt, sugar, milk, and melted butter. Set aside. Bring blackberries, sugar, water, and butter to a boil over medium heat in a wide 2-quart saucepan with lid. When berries boil, spoon batter over top. Cover tightly. Lower heat and simmer without lifting cover for 12 minutes. Biscuit is cooked when knife inserted in center comes out clean. Serve hot with heavy cream. *Serves 4 to 6.*

MENU

Venison Diane

Special Baked Potatoes

Watercress Salad

Peach Melba

VENISON DIANE

2 *boneless venison rib steaks, cut ½ inch thick*
4 *tablespoons butter*
¼ *cup chopped scallions*
2 *tablespoons chopped fresh chives*
1 *tablespoon chopped fresh parsley*
1 *tablespoon Worcestershire sauce*
1 *tablespoon A-1 Sauce*
  Salt to taste
¼ *teaspoon freshly ground black pepper*

Cut the steaks horizontally through the middle, leaving them connected at one side. Open the steaks like a book and pound lightly to flatten.

Melt 2 tablespoons butter in a large skillet over medium heat. Sauté scallions for 5 minutes. Add the steaks. Raise heat and sear

191

quickly on both sides. Add the chives, parsley, Worcestershire sauce, A-1 Sauce, and remaining butter. Stir well and turn steaks. Sprinkle with salt and pepper. Serve immediately. *Serves 2.*

SPECIAL BAKED POTATOES

4 ✱ 5

2 large Idaho potatoes, washed and dried
1 tablespoon vegetable oil
2 tablespoons butter
2 tablespoons sour cream
1 tablespoon chopped fresh chives
1 tablespoon grated Parmesan cheese
  Salt and pepper to taste
1 tablespoon melted butter

Preheat oven to 375°. Coat potatoes with vegetable oil. Bake at 375° for approximately 45 minutes or until pulp is soft when pierced with knife.

Remove from oven. Split in half lengthwise. Scoop out pulp. Whip potatoes with butter, sour cream, chives, grated cheese, salt, and pepper. When well mixed, put back into shells. Brush with melted butter and return to oven to heat through. Serve immediately. *Serves 2.* (4)

WATERCRESS SALAD

1 bunch watercress, washed, dried, and trimmed of tough stalks
1 cup cubed fresh papaya
1 tablespoon toasted pine nuts
¼ cup virgin olive oil
1 tablespoon fresh orange juice
2 tablespoons fruit vinegar
  Salt and pepper to taste

Mix together the watercress, papaya, and pine nuts. Whisk together the olive oil, orange juice, vinegar, salt, and pepper. Toss with salad. Serve immediately. *Serves 2.*

PEACH MELBA

1 cup fresh chopped peaches
1 teaspoon Grand Marnier
½ cup raspberry purée
1 tablespoon sugar
1 pint vanilla ice cream
4 tablespoons whipped cream

Soak chopped peaches with Grand Marnier for 1 hour. Blend raspberry pureé and sugar. Layer peaches, raspberry purée and vanilla ice cream in iced parfait glasses until all used. Sprinkle with raspberry purée and top with whipped cream. Serve immediately. *Serves 2.*

MENU

Amidzich Seven-Layer Loaf

*Baked Tomatoes
with Onions*

Mushroom Soufflé

Florida Pie

AMIDZICH SEVEN-LAYER LOAF

3 pounds venison, ground
3 pounds wild boar, ground (may substitute ground pork)
3 pounds elk, ground
1 pound smoked Canadian ham, ground
2 pounds onions, thinly sliced
  Paprika
  Salt and pepper to taste

Grind your own meat. Cut off rough meat. Keep meat in elongated strands so that when the layers cook juice will flow more easily. Do not pat meat into a ball. Select a large brazier or pan with a lip to build layered loaf on.

Spread a layer of onions in bottom of pan. Add 1½ pounds of venison and liberally sprinkle with paprika, salt, and pepper. Add another layer of onions, a layer of ham, and then 1½ pounds elk meat. Season with paprika, salt, and pepper. Add a layer of onions, ham, and 1½ pounds of wild boar meat, season with paprika, salt, and black pepper. Continue the process until all ingredients are used.

When the loaf is complete, cover entire top with paprika, salt, and black pepper. This will help seal in the juices and create a glaze on the outside. Insert meat thermometer. Cover and place on the top of prepared charcoal grill. Cook, basting every 30 minutes, for about 4 hours or until meat thermometer registers done. *Serves 10 to 12.*

NOTE: This recipe is great for a summer party.

BAKED TOMATOES WITH ONIONS

2 dozen pearl onions
7 cups cooked tomatoes
  Salt and pepper to taste
¼ cup brown sugar
½ cup bread crumbs
¼ cup butter

Preheat oven to 325°. Peel onions and drop into boiling water. Parboil 20 minutes. Drain. Combine tomatoes, salt, pepper, and sugar and turn into casserole. Place onions in center. Sprinkle with bread crumbs and dot with butter. Bake, uncovered, at 325° about 20 minutes or until bubbling and brown. *Serves 12.*

MUSHROOM SOUFFLÉ

1 pound fresh mushrooms, sliced
½ cup butter, melted
10 slices bread, buttered, cut into 1-inch slices
½ cup finely chopped onion
½ cup finely chopped celery
½ cup finely chopped green pepper
½ cup mayonnaise
2 eggs, beaten
1½ cups milk
   Salt and pepper to taste
1 can cream of mushroom soup
1 cup grated cheddar cheese

In heavy skillet over medium heat, sauté sliced mushrooms in melted butter until juices run and mushrooms are wilted. Set aside. Place half of the bread in a 2-quart greased baking dish. Combine mushrooms, onions, celery, green pepper, and mayonnaise. Spoon over bread. Top with half of remaining bread. Combine eggs, milk, salt, and pepper. Pour over bread and refrigerate two hours.

Preheat oven to 300°. Spread soup over top and cover with remaining bread cubes. Bake at 300° for 40 minutes. Remove from heat and add cheese. Bake 20 minutes longer. Serve immediately. *Serves 10 to 12.*

FLORIDA PIE

½ cup sugar
4 tablespoons flour
1 cup orange juice
1 tablespoon lemon juice
3 egg yolks, beaten
1 teaspoon butter
½ cup drained crushed pineapple
1 Graham Cracker Pie Shell
1 recipe Marshmallow Meringue
½ cup moist shredded coconut

Preheat oven to 450°. Mix sugar and flour together in top half of double boiler over boiling water. Add fruit juices and cook for 10 minutes, stirring occasionally. Slowly add to egg yolks, return to heat and cook 15 minutes over boiling water, stirring constantly. Remove from heat. Stir in butter and pineapple. Cool. Pour into Graham Cracker Pie Shell. Cover with meringue. Sprinkle with coconut and bake for 2 minutes at 450° or until light brown. *Serves 6.*

GRAHAM CRACKER PIE SHELL

1½ cups fine graham cracker crumbs
¼ cup sugar
½ cup melted butter

Mix crumbs and sugar together. Stir in butter. Line pie pan by pressing mixture firmly into place. Chill for 20 minutes, or bake in moderate 350° oven for 10 minutes. Cool. *Makes one 9-inch shell.*

MARSHMALLOW MERINGUE

12 marshmallows
1 tablespoon milk
2 egg whites
¼ cup sugar
¼ teaspoon salt
½ teaspoon vanilla

In a small saucepan over low heat, melt marshmallows with milk; fold together until marshmallows are half melted. Remove from heat and continue folding until mixture is smooth and fluffy. Beat egg whites, add sugar gradually, and continue beating until stiff. Add salt and vanilla. Blend into marshmallow mixture and spread over pie. *Makes enough for one 9-inch pie.*

MENU

❦

Venison
with Mustard Sauce

Basil Beans

Potato Pancakes

Rice Tart

VENISON WITH MUSTARD SAUCE

> 8 thin slices venison (about ¾ pound)
> ⅓ cup flour
>   Salt and pepper to taste
> 4 tablespoons butter
> 2 tablespoons minced shallots
> ¼ cup dry white wine
> ½ cup heavy cream
> 1 tablespoon Dijon mustard

Pound venison slices with a mallet until very thin. Blend flour, salt, and pepper. Dredge meat on both sides.

Heat butter in heavy skillet over very hot heat; do not brown. Add venison. Sear quickly until golden brown, about 2 minutes on each side. Remove from skillet and keep warm.

Add shallots to skillet and sauté 3 minutes. Add wine and cook until it is almost totally evaporated. Add cream and bring to a boil. Cook about 30 seconds; remove from heat. Stir in mustard but do not cook further.

Spoon sauce over the meat. Serve with fine buttered noodles. *Serves 4.*

BASIL BEANS

1 *pound fresh green beans, washed and trimmed*
3 *tablespoons butter*
⅓ *cup cracker crumbs*
½ *teaspoon minced fresh basil*
 Salt and pepper to taste

Steam beans until done but still crisp. In a small skillet over medium heat, melt butter. Add crumbs and sauté for 2 minutes at medium low heat. Add basil, salt, and pepper; toss with beans. *Serves 4 to 6.*

POTATO PANCAKES

4 *medium potatoes*
½ *cup grated onion*
1 *egg*
2 *tablespoons flour*
 Salt and pepper to taste
¼ *cup vegetable oil, approximately*

Peel potatoes. Grate. Mix with onion, egg, flour, salt, and pepper.

In a heavy skillet, pour enough oil to cover bottom. Heat to sizzling. Drop potatoes by the heaping spoonful into oil. Fry, turning once, until golden on both sides. Drain on paper towel. Serve hot. Serve with a garnish of sour cream and/or apple sauce, if desired. *Serves 4 to 6.*

RICE TART

¾ cup rice
3 cups milk
½ teaspoon salt
4 egg yolks
1 cup sugar
½ teaspoon vanilla
¼ cup rum
1 cup heavy cream, whipped
1 9-inch baked pie shell (see Plain Pastry, page 8)
Cinnamon

Wash rice in cold water. Heat milk, add salt and rice, and cook over low heat for about 50 minutes or until tender, stirring occasionally. Beat egg yolks, add sugar and combine with rice. Cook 1 minute longer. Cool. Fold in vanilla, rum, and whipped cream. Fill baked pastry shell. Sprinkle with cinnamon and brown under broiler. *Serves 4 to 6.*

NOTE: Omit rum and vanilla if desired, and flavor with 1 tablespoon lemon juice.

OTHER RECIPES

❧

VENISON WITH CAPERS AND CREAM

6 venison loin chops, about ¾ inch thick
2 tablespoons butter
2 tablespoons olive oil
    Salt and freshly ground pepper to taste
2 tablespoons minced shallots
½ cup beef broth
¼ cup dry vermouth
1 tablespoon fresh lemon juice
½ cup heavy cream
2 tablespoons capers, rinsed and drained
2 tablespoons minced fresh parsley

Pat venison dry with paper towels. Melt butter and oil in large heavy skillet over medium heat. Add venison (in batches if necessary; do not crowd) and brown on one side. Turn chops and season with salt and pepper. Continue cooking until just springy to touch and pink in center, about 7 minutes. Transfer to heated platter. Cover and keep warm.

Pour off all but 2 tablespoons fat in skillet. Add shallots and cook for 2 minutes. Add broth, vermouth, and lemon juice; boil until reduced by half, scraping up any brown bits. Stir in cream and capers. Simmer for about 5 minutes, or until thick. Adjust seasoning. Pour sauce over warm venison. Sprinkle with parsley and serve. *Serves 6.*

SPICED VENISON

    1 5-pound venison roast, boned
    3 ounces rock salt
    ½ ounce saltpeter
    1 teaspoon cloves, ground
    1 teaspoon ginger
    1 teaspoon mace
    1 tablespoon black pepper
    1½ teaspoons ground allspice
    3 ounces brown sugar
    1 onion
    2 stalks celery
    1 carrot

Mix half the rock salt and the saltpeter; rub well into boned meat. Place in earthenware crock. Cover and let stand for 24 hours. Mix spices together and rub into venison.

Place venison back in the crock and sprinkle with a mixture of remaining salts and sugar. Cover and let stand for 5 days, turning daily. A liquid will form as the meat pickles and should be used daily to baste meat.

After 5 days, remove the meat and wash well in cold water. Roll and tie securely. Place in Dutch oven and cover with cold water. Place over low heat and bring to a boil. Add the vegetables and simmer for 3 hours, or until the meat is tender. Let meat cool in the liquid. When cool, remove and press with a weight. Slice and serve. *Serves 6.*

BROILED VENISON STEAK

    2 pounds venison steak, 1 inch thick
    1 clove garlic
    2 tablespoons fat, melted
    4 large mushroom caps
       Salt and pepper
       Parsley and/or watercress, for garnish

Preheat broiler. Rub steak on both sides with garlic and brush with fat. Place on greased broiler rack in preheated broiler and broil for 5 minutes. Turn and brush with fat and broil on other side. Broil

pierce meat with 202 a sharp 2 tine for every inch. both sides & rub in a little meat tenderizer. Works every time.

mushroom caps. Season steak with salt and pepper and garnish with mushroom caps, parsley and/or watercress. *Serves 4.*

JENNIFER WILCOX'S VENISON ROAST   *Do*

1 4-pound venison roast
1 teaspoon garlic salt
1 teaspoon onion salt
2 teaspoons celery salt
1½ teaspoons salt
2 teaspoons Worcestershire sauce
2 teaspoons pepper
1 tablespoon liquid smoke   *use any game*
3 tablespoons brown sugar
1 tablespoon dry mustard   *or pork.*
   Dash of ground nutmeg
1 tablespoon soy sauce
1 tablespoon fresh lemon juice
3 drops Tabasco sauce
½ cup catsup (*cranberry sauce*)

Preheat oven to 300°. Place venison in roasting pan. Combine all ingredients and pour over meat. Cover and bake at 300° for about 4 hours or until tender; baste frequently. *Serves 6.*

YANKEE VENISON POT ROAST

1 4- to 6-pound venison roast
¼ pound salt pork or fat bacon
2 medium celery stalks, sliced
2 carrots, peeled and sliced
1 small onion, sliced
1 1-pound can tomatoes
2 teaspoons salt
6 peppercorns
1 bay leaf
3 cups water
¼ cup flour
⅓ cup each cooked peas, cubed carrots, and cut string beans
½ cup cooked, chopped celery

In a Dutch oven, brown roast in salt pork or fat bacon over medium heat. Put celery, carrots, onion slices and tomatoes around meat. Add salt, peppercorns, bay leaf, and water. Bring to a boil. Reduce heat; cover and simmer over low heat (or in a 350° oven) for 2½ hours. Remove from heat. Lift out roast; keep warm.

Strain stock, discarding vegetables. Skim fat off stock, returning ¼ cup fat to Dutch oven. Stir in flour. Add 4 cups stock and cook, stirring constantly, until thick. Check seasonings. Add vegetables and heat through. Slice venison, surround with vegetables and drizzle on gravy. Serve extra gravy on the side. *Serves 8 to 12.*

Wolf River Stuffed Cabbage

2 *pounds ground venison*
1½ *tablespoons salt*
1½ *tablespoons black pepper*
¼ *teaspoon garlic powder*
1 *egg*
1 *cup raw rice*
1 *large green cabbage*

SAUCE

3 *cans tomato soup*
2½ *cups water*
1 *can stewed tomatoes*
1 *bay leaf*
½ *teaspoon lemon juice*
1 *12-ounce can sauerkraut*

Preheat oven to 350°. Mix together the ground venison, seasonings, egg, and rice. Cover and set aside.

Core cabbage. Place in deep pot, cover with boiling water, and let stand until leaves can be easily removed from head and are pliable.

Dry each leaf and fill with meat mixture. Roll up, folding ends in and over mixture as you roll. Secure with toothpicks.

Place in large Dutch oven. Mix together all ingredients for sauce and pour over cabbage rolls. Cover and bake at 350° for 2 hours. Serve immediately. *Serves 8.*·

MENU
❧

Cold Artichoke Vinaigrette

Florida Beach Buck
with Coconut and Brown Rice

Papaya Pepper Salad

Carrot Torte

COLD ARTICHOKE VINAIGRETTE

8 artichokes
1 lemon, quartered
  Salt to taste
1 recipe Manion Vinaigrette (see page 40)
2 tablespoons grated Parmesan cheese

Trim the top and stem from each artichoke. Using kitchen shears, trim the points off outer leaves. Wash well.

Place the artichokes in a heavy saucepan with water to cover. Add the lemon quarters and salt to taste. Bring to a boil, cover, and cook for approximately 40 minutes or until they are just tender. Remove from water. Drain, upside down, until cool.

When well drained and cool, place in individual salad bowls and cover with vinaigrette. Sprinkle with grated cheese. *Serves 8.*

FLORIDA BEACH BUCK WITH COCONUT

1 2½-pound sirloin steak, cut ¼ inch thick (round steak may be
  substituted)
2 cups milk
1 cup shredded coconut
1½ teaspoons flour
  Salt and pepper to taste
3 tablespoons vegetable oil
1 teaspoon sugar
¼ teaspoon finely chopped chili pepper
¾ cup dry-roasted peanuts
4 cloves garlic, minced
½ cup chopped onions
2 teaspoons grated lemon rind
2 tablespoons cornstarch
¼ cup heavy cream
1 8-ounce can water chestnuts

Combine milk and coconut in a saucepan. Bring to a boil over medium heat. Remove from the heat and let stand 30 minutes. Strain off liquid. Cut up meat into small cubes. Coat with flour, salt, and pepper. Shake off excess. Heat oil in a heavy skillet over medium heat. Add meat and cook for about 20 minutes, turning frequently until all sides are brown.

Add coconut milk and simmer for about 30 minutes over very low heat. In a blender or food processor, combine sugar, chili pepper, peanuts, garlic, onion, and lemon rind. Blend into the simmering meat.

Mix the cornstarch and cream together until combined. Add to meat and bring to a boil, stirring constantly. Immediately reduce heat and simmer for 5 minutes.

Slice the water chestnuts and cook them in their liquid for 5 minutes. Drain and place on heated serving platter and cover with meat and sauce. Serve immediately with brown rice. *Serves 6 to 8.*

PAPAYA PEPPER SALAD

2½ cups diced fresh papaya
1½ cups diced fresh pineapple
 1 cup sliced celery
 2 tablespoons finely chopped onion
 1 cup plain yogurt
 ¼ cup white wine vinegar
 2 teaspoons fresh lemon juice
 ½ teaspoon grated onion
 1 teaspoon freshly cracked black pepper
 1 head red leaf lettuce

Mix together the fruit, celery, and chopped onion. Stir in yogurt, vinegar, lemon juice, grated onion, and pepper. Toss to blend. Cover and refrigerate for 30 minutes before serving. On a bed of red leaf lettuce, place equal portions of papaya salad on salad plates. Add a dash of cracked pepper on top. *Serves 6 to 8.*

CARROT TORTE

 8 eggs, separated
 2 cups sugar
 1 tablespoon fresh orange juice
   Grated rind of 1 orange
 1 pound carrots, grated
 1 pound almonds, blanched and chopped fine

Preheat oven to 350°. Beat egg yolks until thick and light yellow. Beat in sugar gradually. Add orange juice and rind. Add carrots and nuts. Beat egg whites until stiff and fold into the batter. Pour into greased torte pan and bake at 350° for 50 minutes. Chill. Unmold and serve with whipped cream. *Serves 8 to 12.*

MENU

O'Manion Potted Elk Roast

Cucumber-Beet Salad

Cheese Crescents

Harvest Pudding

O'MANION POTTED ELK ROAST

1 3- to 4-pound elk rump roast
3 tablespoons butter
½ pound potatoes, peeled and cut into chunks
½ pound carrots, peeled and cut into chunks
½ pound onions, peeled and sliced
¼ green pepper, seeded and cut into cubes
1 package onion soup mix
Salt and pepper to taste
¼ cup red wine
½ cup water
2 tablespoons flour

Trim all fat and silverskin from meat. Melt butter in heavy skillet over medium heat. Brown meat on four sides. Remove meat from skillet and place in a large crock pot. Add remaining ingredients, except flour. Cook on low for 8 hours or until meat falls apart with a fork.

Remove meat and vegetables to serving platter. Keep warm. Blend flour into 1 cup broth. Place in saucepan with remaining broth and bring to a boil. Cook, stirring constantly, for 2 to 3 minutes, or until thick. Serve with sliced meat and vegetables. *Serves 4 to 6.*

CUCUMBER-BEET SALAD

2 *cups sliced peeled cucumbers*
1 *cup grated raw beets*
2 *tablespoons chopped fresh dill*
2 *tablespoons chopped scallions*
1 *tablespoon sugar*
½ *cup vinegar*
  Salt and pepper to taste

Mix all ingredients together. Cover and refrigerate at least 3 hours before serving. *Serves 4 to 6.*

CHEESE CRESCENTS

2 *cups flour*
1 *tablespoon baking powder*
¼ *teaspoon salt*
½ *cup butter*
½ *cup grated Parmesan cheese*
¾ *cup light cream*
3 *tablespoons melted butter*
2 *teaspoons cracked black pepper*

Preheat oven to 400°. Sift together flour, baking powder, and salt. Place in food processor bowl; using the metal blade, cut in the butter and ¼ cup Parmesan cheese until crumbly. Add cream and knead until dough sticks together. Add more flour if necessary.

Remove mixture from bowl and roll out a 12-inch circle on a lightly floured board. Brush with 2 tablespoons melted butter, remaining ¼ cup grated cheese, and cracked pepper.

209

Cut into 12 equal wedges. Roll up, from the top, and curve into crescent shapes. Place on a greased cookie sheet and brush with 1 tablespoon melted butter. Bake at 400° for 2 minutes or until golden. Serve hot. *Serves 4 to 6.*

HARVEST PUDDING

3½ cups tart apples, sliced
½ cup raisins
¾ cup sugar
½ teaspoon cinnamon
¼ teaspoon nutmeg
¾ cup chopped walnuts
1 teaspoon butter
1 teaspoon lemon juice
½ cup sugar
1¼ cups flour
1 teaspoon baking powder
¼ teaspoon salt
½ cup milk
1 egg
3 tablespoons butter or margarine, melted

Preheat oven to 375°. Place apples and raisins in a well-greased 8-by-13-inch baking pan. Combine sugar, spices, and ½ cup walnuts; sprinkle over fruit. Dot with butter and lemon juice. Sift dry ingredients together. Combine milk, egg, and butter. Add to dry ingredients. Mix until smooth. Pour over the fruit and sprinkle with remaining walnuts. Bake at 375° for 30 minutes. Serve hot with ice cream or whipped cream sprinkled with cinnamon. *Serves 4 to 8.*

MENU

Elk Chops Rio Grande

Jack Pine Lemon Potatoes

Zucchini Casserole

Fresh Fruit and Sour Cream

ELK CHOPS RIO GRANDE

    6 *elk chops, cut ³⁄₄ inch thick and pounded lightly*
 1¹⁄₂ *teaspoons salt*
  ¹⁄₂ *teaspoon freshly ground black pepper*
    3 *tablespoons olive oil*
  ¹⁄₂ *cup chopped mushrooms*
  ³⁄₄ *cup minced onions*
  ³⁄₄ *cup dry white wine*
  ¹⁄₂ *cup canned tomato sauce*
    2 *teaspoons unsweetened cocoa*
  ¹⁄₄ *teaspoon saffron*
  ¹⁄₄ *cup ground almonds*

Preheat oven to 325°. Trim the fat from the chops and rub them with salt and pepper. Heat oil in a skillet over medium heat. Brown the chops on both sides. Transfer to a baking dish in a single layer and sprinkle with mushrooms. Add onions to oil remaining in the skillet. Sauté for 10 minutes. Add wine and tomato sauce. Cook over low heat for 10 minutes. Stir in cocoa, saffron, and almonds. Taste for seasoning. Pour over chops. Cover and bake at 325° for 40 minutes, removing the cover for the last 5 minutes. *Serves 6.*

JACK PINE LEMON POTATOES

6 cups peeled, 1/8-inch-thick sliced potatoes
6 tablespoons butter, melted
4 tablespoons lemon juice
1/2 teaspoon salt
1/4 teaspoon paprika
Twig of pine needles, for garnish

Preheat oven to 325°. Cover potatoes with cold water and allow to stand for 15 minutes. Drain and place in a saucepan. Cover with boiling salted water. Cook for 2 minutes over medium heat. Drain well and spread in a buttered baking dish.

Bake at 325° for 1 hour or until potatoes are soft. While baking, combine melted butter, lemon juice, salt, and paprika, and baste the potatoes with the mixture three times. Garnish with pine needles, if possible. *Serves 6.*

ZUCCHINI CASSEROLE

1 pound zucchini, trimmed and scrubbed
Pinch of chopped fresh dill
1 clove garlic
Boiling salted water
3 tablespoons butter
1/2 pound mushrooms, sliced
2 tablespoons flour
1 cup sour cream
Salt and pepper to taste
1/2 cup buttered bread crumbs

Preheat broiler. Cut the zucchini crosswise into 1-inch slices. Place in medium saucepan, and add the dill, garlic, and boiling salted water to cover. Bring to a boil again. Reduce heat, cover, and simmer gently for about 5 minutes or until the vegetables are just tender. Do not overcook! Drain, reserving 2 tablespoons of the cooking liquid. Discard garlic.

Melt butter in small skillet over medium heat. Add mushrooms and sauté for 5 minutes, stirring occasionally. Stir in flour and cook 2 minutes longer. Add sour cream, zucchini, and reserved cooking liquid, stirring constantly. Season to taste and heat thoroughly, but do not boil. Transfer to a buttered 2-quart casserole. Top with buttered bread crumbs. Brown quickly under broiler. Serve immediately. *Serves 6.*

FRESH FRUIT AND SOUR CREAM

> 2 *cups sour cream*
> 1½ *cups fresh pineapple pieces*
> 1 *cup tangerine sections*
> 1 *banana, sliced*
> 1 *mandarin orange, sectioned*
> 1 *cup seedless grapes*
> 1 *tablespoon Grand Marnier, optional*
> ½ *cup chopped toasted almonds*

Mix together the sour cream, fruit, and Grand Marnier. Cover and refrigerate for 12 hours. Serve cold topped with toasted almonds. *Serves 6.*

OTHER RECIPES

❧

Denver Elk with Blue Cheese

> 1 4-pound elk round steak, cut 1½ inches thick
> Salt and freshly ground black pepper to taste
> ¾ cup butter
> 1 cup sliced mushrooms
> 2 teaspoons brandy
> ½ cup blue cheese

Preheat broiler. Trim fat from the steak. Broil steak 8 minutes on each side or to desired degree of rareness. Sprinkle with salt and pepper when turning. Heat ¼ cup butter in small skillet over medium heat. Add sliced mushrooms and sauté for about 15 minutes or until juices are reduced to half. Stir in brandy and cook for 1 minute. Set aside.

Mash blue cheese and remaining ½ cup butter together until smooth. When steak is done, immediately spread it with the cheese mixture so that it melts slightly and garnish with mushrooms. *Serves 6 to 8.*

Kaibab Elk with Raisin-Nut Sauce

> 12 elk fillets, cut 1 inch thick
> ½ cup butter
> 3 slices Canadian ham, diced
> ¾ cup chopped mushrooms
> 2 tablespoons Lambrusco wine
> 1 tablespoon flour
> 1 cup beef broth
> ¼ cup pine nuts or slivered almonds
> 1 tablespoon seedless raisins
> ½ cup flour
> Salt and pepper to taste

Trim fat from the meat. Melt 2 tablespoons butter in a skillet over medium heat. Sauté the ham for 3 minutes. Remove and set aside. Add 3 tablespoons butter to the skillet and sauté mushrooms for 3 minutes. Return the ham to skillet and add wine. Cook over medium heat for 3 minutes. Whisk the 1 tablespoon flour into broth and pour into the skillet. Bring to a boil, stirring constantly. Mix in the nuts and raisins. Reduce heat and cook for 10 minutes.

Dip the beef slices in a mixture of ½ cup flour, salt, and pepper. Melt the remaining butter in a skillet over medium heat. Quickly brown the meat on both sides. Add sauce, scraping the meat glaze from the bottom. Cook 2 minutes longer. Transfer to a heated serving dish. *Serves 6 to 8.*

ELK TENDERLOIN WITH BRANDY MUSTARD SAUCE

2 elk tenderloins (8 to 10 ounces each)
1 garlic clove, peeled and cut in half
   Thyme
   Freshly ground black pepper
2 slices raw bacon
½ cup sliced mushrooms
¼ cup onion, finely diced
¼ cup bell pepper, finely diced
¼ cup brandy
½ cup brown gravy
1 tablespoon Dijon mustard

Remove silverskin from tenderloins and rub meat with split garlic clove. Sprinkle lightly with thyme and black pepper. Wrap bacon around tenderloin and use toothpick to secure. Place in hot frying pan and sauté until bacon is well cooked. Tenderloin should not be cooked beyond medium rare. Remove from pan. Keep warm. Add mushrooms, onion, and pepper and sauté until tender.

Add brandy to hot pan and flame. (Use caution.) When flame dies, add brown gravy and mustard and stir until mixture is smooth. Pour mixture over tenderloin on warm platter. Serve with wild rice or pilaf and green vegetables. *Serves 2.*

MENU
❧

Alaskan Moose Pepper Steak

Tossed Green Salad
with Manion Vinaigrette (see page 40)

Old South Batter Bread

Alaska Banana Bread Pudding

ALASKAN MOOSE PEPPER STEAK

1 pound moose backstrap, or steak, sliced very thin
1 teaspoon meat tenderizer, optional
2 tablespoons vegetable oil
2 bell peppers, seeded and chopped
1 cup chopped onions or scallions
1½ cups slivered celery
1 tablespoon cornstarch
1½ teaspoons ground ginger
4 tablespoons soy sauce
2 teaspoons lemon juice
1¼ cups water
½ cup light molasses

Sprinkle the sliced steak with meat tenderizer, if needed. Heat the oil in a heavy skillet or wok over medium heat. Add the venison and cook only until red color disappears. Add the peppers and sauté lightly. Add the onions and celery and sauté for 3 minutes. Blend cornstarch and ginger with the soy sauce, lemon juice, water, and molasses. Add to meat and cook, stirring constantly, until thick. Serve over hot rice. *Serves 4.*

OLD SOUTH BATTER BREAD

½ *cup white water-ground cornmeal*
1½ *cups milk*
1 *tablespoon butter, melted*
¾ *teaspoon salt*
2 *eggs*
1½ *teaspoons baking powder*

Preheat oven to 400°. In a medium saucepan mix together the cornmeal, 1 cup milk, melted butter, and salt. Bring to a boil over medium heat, stirring constantly. Remove from heat and cool.

Beat together ½ cup milk and eggs. Stir into cooled cornmeal. When well blended, whisk in baking powder.

Pour into buttered 1½-quart casserole. Bake, at 400° for 35 minutes or until crust is golden brown. Serve hot with lots of fresh butter. *Serves 4 to 8.*

ALASKA BANANA BREAD PUDDING

2 *bananas, mashed*
1 *cup granulated sugar*
2½ *cups milk*
¼ *cup sweet sherry*
¼ *teaspoon grated nutmeg*
4 *eggs, lightly beaten*
3 *cups dry bread crumbs*
½ *cup diced citron*
2 *tablespoons butter*

Preheat oven to 350°. Mix the bananas, sugar, milk, sherry, and nutmeg together. Beat in the eggs. Add bread crumbs and

217

citron. Blend thoroughly and pour into a buttered 1½-quart casserole. Dot top with butter.

Bake, uncovered, at 350° for 1 hour, or until the pudding is nicely puffed and brown and the top is firm when lightly touched in the center. Serve cold or at room temperature with whipped cream or ice cream. *Serves 4 to 8.*

OTHER RECIPES

❧

TERRY COX'S BARBECUE MOOSE ROAST IN A POT

    1 4-pound rump, round, or chuck moosemeat roast
    2 tablespoons vegetable oil
    1 cup tomato sauce
    ½ cup cider vinegar
      Salt and pepper to taste
    2 teaspoons chili powder
    ¼ teaspoon paprika
    2 tablespoons vegetable oil (additional, if needed)

Heat oil in Dutch oven over medium heat. Brown meat on all
sides. Mix together the tomato sauce, vinegar, salt, pepper, chili
powder, and paprika. Put browned meat and sauce in a large crock
pot and cook for 8 hours. Turn meat several times during cooking.
Add water, if necessary, to keep meat from sticking.

If moose lacks fat, add 2 tablespoons salad oil to the tomato
sauce mixture. For a thicker gravy, remove meat to a serving platter,
and mix 1 tablespoon flour and 2 tablespoons water to a smooth
paste; stir into the liquid in the kettle. Serve with sliced meat. *Serves
6 to 8.*

MENU

❧

Herb Charcoal Antelope Steak

American Fried Potatoes (see page 132)

Picnic Salad

Countryside Johnnycake

Brownies

HERB CHARCOAL ANTELOPE STEAK

3 pounds antelope round steak, cut 1½ inches thick
¾ cup fresh lemon juice
½ cup chopped onion
¼ cup vegetable oil
½ teaspoon vegetable oil
½ teaspoon salt
½ teaspoon celery seed
½ teaspoon onion salt
½ teaspoon thyme, if desired
½ teaspoon rosemary
½ teaspoon oregano, if desired
2 cloves garlic, crushed

In plastic bag or large shallow bowl, combine all ingredients except meat. Add meat and marinate 6 to 8 hours. Prepare barbecue

220

for cooking. Place steak on rack 6 inches above hot coals. Grill 10 to 15 minutes, basting occasionally. Turn, continue basting, and grill 10 to 15 minutes longer for medium steak. *Serves 6 to 8.*

PICNIC SALAD

3 cups cooked lima beans
½ cup finely chopped sweet pickle
½ cup finely cut celery
½ cup chopped stuffed olives
1 recipe Horseradish Cream Dressing
  Salt and pepper to taste
1 head chicory

Toss first six ingredients together lightly. Chill for at least an hour before serving. Place bed of chicory on each salad plate and place bean salad in center. Serve immediately. *Serves 8.*

HORSERADISH CREAM DRESSING

1 cup heavy cream
1 tablespoon lemon juice
1 tablespoon tarragon vinegar
1 tablespoon red wine vinegar
3 tablespoons grated fresh horseradish
  Dash of salt
  Dash of sugar
¼ teaspoon prepared mustard

Whip cream. Gradually add lemon juice and vinegar. Blend in horseradish, salt, sugar, and mustard. *Makes 2 cups.*

NOTE: Two tablespoons grated cucumber may be added for variety.

COUNTRYSIDE JOHNNYCAKE

1½ cups milk
1 tablespoon lemon juice
2 cups yellow cornmeal
1 cup all-purpose flour
1½ teaspoons granulated sugar
½ teaspoon salt
3 tablespoons butter
3 tablespoons vegetable shortening
1 egg, separated
1 teaspoon baking soda
2 tablespoons hot water

Preheat oven to 350°. Mix milk with lemon juice and set in a warm oven for a few minutes to sour. Combine the cornmeal, flour, sugar, and salt. Cut in the butter and shortening until crumbly.

Stir the egg yolk into the dry ingredients along with the soured milk. Dissolve the baking soda in the hot water and add. Mix well.

Beat the egg white until stiff and fold into the batter. Pour the batter into a greased 8-inch square pan and bake at 350° for 35 minutes, or until lightly browned. Cut into squares and serve hot, dripping with butter. *Serves 4 to 8.*

BROWNIES

1 cup butter
1 cup white sugar
1 cup brown sugar
4 eggs
4 squares unsweetened baking chocolate, melted
1 cup flour
½ teaspoon baking powder
1 teaspoon vanilla
1 cup walnut or pecan pieces

Preheat oven to 325°. Cream butter and sugars until light and fluffy. Add eggs and melted chocolate. Sift together flour and baking powder and stir into batter. When well mixed, add vanilla and nuts.

Pour into greased and floured 9-by-14-inch baking pan. Bake at 325° for 30 minutes or until top is a bit glazed and sides are pulling away from pan. Remove from heat. Cool on wire rack. When cool, cut into squares. *Serves 4 to 8.*

MENU
❧

Southern-Style Antelope Chops

Potatoes and Cabbage
with Cheese Sauce

Carrot Slaw

Settler's First Indian Pudding

SOUTHERN-STYLE ANTELOPE CHOPS

6 *antelope chops, cut ¾ inch thick and pounded lightly*
1½ *teaspoons salt*
¼ *teaspoon white pepper*
1½ *cups crushed cornflakes*
2 *eggs*
2 *tablespoons light cream*
2 *tablespoons vegetable oil*
3 *tablespoons butter*

Preheat oven to 325°. Trim fat from the chops. Season with salt and pepper. Dip in cornflakes, then in eggs beaten with cream. Dip again in cornflakes. Heat oil and butter in a skillet (with an oven-proof handle) over medium heat. Brown the chops on both sides. Cover and place in preheated 325° oven. Bake for 15 minutes; turn and bake 15 more minutes or until tender. *Serves 6.*

POTATOES AND CABBAGE WITH CHEESE SAUCE

3 cups diced potatoes
4 cups chopped cabbage
2 cups boiling water
2 teaspoons salt
1 cup light cream
1 cup grated cheddar cheese

Cook potatoes and cabbage uncovered in boiling salted water for 15 minutes or until potatoes are tender. Most of the water should have evaporated when potatoes are cooked. If not, drain and keep warm. Scald cream. Add cheese and stir until melted. Pour cheese sauce over vegetables and serve at once. *Serves 6.*

CARROT SLAW

3 cups grated raw carrots
¼ cup grated raw beets
½ cup grated raw zucchini
½ cup grated Granny Smith apples
2 tablespoons grated onion
1 tablespoon chopped fresh parsley
2 tablespoons chopped sweet red pepper
¼ cup toasted sunflower seeds
½ cup mayonnaise
2 tablespoons white wine vinegar
2 tablespoons sour cream
1 teaspoon minced fresh dill
Salt and pepper to taste

Mix all ingredients together until well blended. Refrigerate, covered, for at least 1 hour before serving. Serve alone or on a bed of lettuce. *Serves 6 to 8.*

SETTLER'S FIRST INDIAN PUDDING

7 cups milk
6 tablespoons butter
¾ cup yellow cornmeal
1 cup sugar
¼ cup molasses
1½ teaspoons salt
1¼ teaspoons ground cinnamon
½ teaspoon grated nutmeg
1 recipe Vanilla Custard (see page 152)

Preheat oven to 300°. Place 5½ cups milk in a saucepan over medium heat. When hot, stir in the butter, cornmeal, sugar, molasses, salt, and spices. Cook, stirring constantly, for about 20 minutes, or until thick.

Pour the pudding into a greased 2-quart casserole. Carefully pour reserved 1½ cups milk on top of the pudding, allowing it to float without stirring it in. Bake at 300° for 3 to 4 hours, or until the pudding is set. Serve hot with Vanilla Custard. *Serves 6 to 10.*

OTHER RECIPES

❧

REINDEER POT ROAST

1 3-pound reindeer pot roast
½ pound salt pork
½ cup flour
  Salt and pepper
1½ cups water
  Salt and pepper to taste
1 bay leaf
4 carrots, peeled and cubed
4 turnips, peeled and cubed
4 potatoes, peeled and cubed
6 small onions

Wipe meat with damp cloth and lard with three-quarters of the salt pork. Rub with flour, salt, and pepper. Fry remaining salt pork in Dutch oven over medium heat. Brown meat on all sides in the fat. Remove meat. Brown 2 tablespoons flour in fat. Set meat on low rack in Dutch oven. Add water and seasonings. Cover and simmer for about 3 hours, or until meat is nearly tender. Place vegetables around and over meat and continue cooking for about 30 minutes or until vegetables are tender. Serve roast, sliced, surrounded with vegetables. Thicken the gravy if necessary with 2 tablespoons flour blended with 2 tablespoons butter and serve with meat. *Serves 4.*

STEAK IN A PACKAGE

2 pounds round steak (moose, caribou, venison, elk) cut 1 inch
  thick
1 cup catsup
¼ cup flour
  Salt and pepper to taste
1 large onion, sliced
2 tablespoons lemon juice or 1 lemon, sliced thin

Preheat oven to 450°. Make a double fold of aluminum foil large enough to enclose steak. Mix catsup and flour together. Place half in center of foil, cover with steak and season with salt and pepper. Add remaining catsup and onion slices; sprinkle with lemon juice or top with lemon slices. Fold foil over and seal securely. Place in shallow baking pan and bake at 450° for 1½ hours, or until done. May also be baked in hot coals of campfire. *Serves 4.*

Chapter Five

EXOTIC BIG GAME

MENU

Boar Chops
with Beer

Parsley Rice and Peas

Hearts of Lettuce
with Dill Dressing

Apple Muffins

BOAR CHOPS WITH BEER

4 ribs or loin boar chops, about 1 inch thick
3 cloves garlic, minced
½ teaspoon caraway seeds
  Salt and pepper to taste
¼ cup flour
2 tablespoons vegetable oil
1 cup beer
1 tablespoon prepared mustard
1 cup beef broth

Rub each chop on both sides with garlic, caraway seeds, salt, and pepper. Dredge in flour. Heat oil in heavy skillet over medium heat and brown chops on both sides. When brown, remove from heat and keep warm.

231

Drain fat from skillet, leaving brown bits in pan. Add beer and bring to a boil over high heat, stirring and scraping skillet to loosen brown bits. Lower heat and simmer until liquid is reduced to ½ cup. Stir in mustard and beef broth. Simmer until sauce is reduced to 1 cup.

Place chops in skillet. Cover and simmer over low heat for 45 minutes, turning once. Serve with sauce. *Serves 4.*

PARSLEY RICE AND PEAS

2 cups cooked rice
1 cup thawed frozen petite peas
¼ tablespoon chopped fresh parsley
1 tablespoon olive oil
  Salt and pepper to taste

Mix all ingredients together in small saucepan over low heat. Cover and heat through, stirring frequently, to keep rice from sticking. *Serves 4.*

HEARTS OF LETTUCE WITH DILL DRESSING

1 small head iceberg lettuce
1 recipe Dill Dressing
1 teaspoon chopped fresh dill

Core, wash, and drain lettuce. Cut into quarters and place each on a salad plate. Cover with Dill Dressing and garnish with chopped fresh dill. *Serves 4.*

DILL DRESSING

½ cup mayonnaise
½ cup sour cream
1 tablespoon heavy cream
2 teaspoons minced onion
2 tablespoons chopped fresh dill
  Salt and pepper to taste

Whisk all ingredients together. Cool and chill for at least 1 hour. *Makes approximately 1 cup.*

APPLE MUFFINS

2 *cups flour*
3/4 *teaspoon salt*
2 *teaspoons baking powder*
4 *tablespoons sugar*
2 *tablespoons butter*
1 *cup peeled and cored finely chopped apples*
1 *egg*
1/2 *cup milk*
12 *apple slices*
1/2 *teaspoon ground cinnamon*

Preheat oven to 400°. Mix flour, salt, baking powder, and 2 tablespoons sugar. Cut in the butter with a fork. Mix in chopped apples. Beat egg with milk and quickly stir into batter. Drop by spoonfuls into greased 12-cup muffin pan. Place one slice of apple on each muffin. Mix remaining sugar with the cinnamon and sprinkle on top. Bake at 400° for about 20 minutes or until light brown. Serve warm. *Makes 12 muffins.*

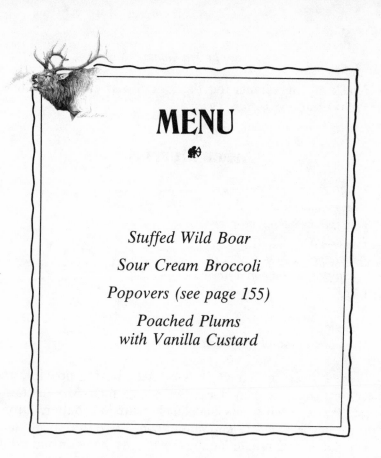

MENU

🐗

Stuffed Wild Boar

Sour Cream Broccoli

Popovers (see page 155)

*Poached Plums
with Vanilla Custard*

STUFFED WILD BOAR

1 4- to 5-pound loin of boar with pocket
1 cup peeled, cored, and cubed apples
1½ cups soft bread cubes
1 teaspoon salt
3 tablespoons sugar
1 small onion, minced
¼ cup hot water
1 cup cranberry sauce, drained
Salt and pepper to taste

Pork loin.

Preheat oven to 325°. Combine apples, bread cubes, salt, sugar, onion, water, and cranberry sauce. Toss lightly to mix. Fill pocket in the meat. Sprinkle with salt and pepper. Place on rack in roasting pan. Bake at 325° for 3 to 3½ hours, or until meat thermometer registers 185°. Serve with additional cranberry sauce. *Serves 8.*

2222222222222222

SOUR CREAM BROCCOLI

1 large head broccoli, steamed
2 tablespoons butter
2 tablespoons minced onion
1½ cups sour cream
1 teaspoon honey
1 teaspoon cider vinegar
½ teaspoon poppy seed
½ teaspoon paprika
¼ teaspoon salt
  Dash of cayenne
⅓ cup chopped cashews

Melt butter in small saucepan over medium heat. Add onion and sauté until soft. Add sour cream, honey, vinegar, poppy seed, paprika, salt, and cayenne. Heat through. Serve on hot, steamed broccoli. Garnish with cashews. *Serves 8.*

POACHED PLUMS WITH VANILLA CUSTARD

2 pounds Italian plums
2 cups dry white wine
½ cup sugar
1 cinnamon stick, broken into bits
4 cloves
1 orange, quartered
1 recipe Vanilla Custard (see page 152)

Wash and dry plums. Place wine, sugar, cinnamon, cloves, and orange quarters in large saucepan over medium heat. Bring to a boil. Lower heat and add plums. Cover and simmer for 15 minutes or until plum skins are just about to burst. Remove from heat and cool.

Remove plums from wine and serve, cold, with Vanilla Custard. Wine may be kept, covered and refrigerated, for cooking other plums for up to 1 month. *Serves 6 to 8.*

MENU

Roast Boar
with Spicy Sauce

Stuffed Peppers

Grapefruit, Avocado, and Spinach Salad

Strawberry Sundaes

ROAST BOAR WITH SPICY SAUCE

1 fresh boar picnic shoulder, boned and rolled
  Salt and pepper to taste
2 small onions, minced
1 tablespoon Worcestershire sauce
1 tablespoon sugar
½ teaspoon paprika
½ cup vinegar
½ cup water
2 tablespoons catsup

Preheat oven to 350°. Season meat with salt and pepper. Place fat side up on rack in open roaster. Roast, at 350°, until meat thermometer registers 185°, or allow 40 to 50 minutes per pound. Combine remaining ingredients in small saucepan and cook over low heat for 5 minutes. Slice roast and serve with sauce. *Serves 6.*

STUFFED PEPPERS

6 green peppers
2¼ cups grated cheddar cheese
2½ cups bread crumbs
1½ teaspoons chopped onion
3 tablespoons butter
Salt and pepper to taste
¼ teaspoon paprika

Preheat oven to 350°. Cut thin slice from stem end of peppers and remove seeds. Parboil peppers 2 minutes in boiling salted water. Drain. Mix together 2 cups cheese, crumbs, onion, butter, salt, pepper, and paprika. When well blended, stuff into well-drained peppers.

Place in greased baking dish, top with remaining cheese, and bake at 350° for 15 minutes. Increase temperature to 425° and bake 5 minutes longer. *Serves 6.*

GRAPEFRUIT, AVOCADO, AND SPINACH SALAD

1 cup fresh grapefruit sections
1 avocado, peeled, seeded, and cubed
6 cups fresh spinach, washed and torn into bite-size pieces
½ cup olive oil
¼ cup walnut oil
3 tablespoons fresh grapefruit juice
3 tablespoons white wine vinegar
1 teaspoon grated orange rind
Salt and pepper to taste

Combine the grapefruit, avocado and spinach. Whisk together the olive oil, walnut oil, grapefruit juice, vinegar, grated orange rind, salt, and pepper. Pour over salad and toss to coat. Serve immediately. *Serves 6.*

STRAWBERRY SUNDAES

6 scoops vanilla or strawberry ice cream
1 recipe Strawberry Sauce
1 cup whipped cream
6 fresh mint sprigs

Place 1 scoop of ice cream in sundae dish. Cover with Strawberry Sauce and garnish with whipped cream and mint sprigs. *Serves 6.*

STRAWBERRY SAUCE

2 cups sliced fresh strawberries
½ cup sugar
1 teaspoon lemon juice
1 tablespoon cornstarch
¼ cup orange juice
2 teaspoons Triple Sec, optional

Combine strawberries, sugar, and lemon juice in small saucepan over medium heat. Bring to a boil. Lower heat and add cornstarch dissolved in orange juice. Cook, stirring constantly, until thick. Remove from heat and stir in Triple Sec. Serve warm or cold over ice cream or fresh, rich pudding. *Makes approximately 3 cups.*

MENU

Marinated Javelina Chops

Fried Rice

Crispy Salad

Caramel Custard

MARINATED JAVELINA CHOPS

8 thin javelina chops, or 4 thicker chops
4 tablespoons soy sauce
2 tablespoons orange juice
2 tablespoons olive oil or corn oil
2 tablespoons tomato catsup
2 tablespoons light brown sugar
1 teaspoon ground ginger
  Grated rind of 1 orange
  Salt and freshly ground black pepper to taste
  Small bunch scallions, thinly sliced

Place 4 chops in a dish so they do not overlap one another. Mix remaining ingredients together, stirring to dissolve sugar. Spoon over half the marinade, putting a few pieces of scallion on each chop. Put the additional chops on top and pour on the remaining

239

marinade. Cover and refrigerate at least 6 hours, basting occasionally.

Preheat broiler. Remove chops and reserve marinade. Broil under high heat about 4 minutes on each side. (Thicker chops will need about 7 to 8 minutes each side.) Spoon the marinade onto the chops when you turn them, so that the scallions become brown and crispy. Serve at once on a warmed serving plate. *Serves 4.*

FRIED RICE

2 tablespoons peanut oil
3 cups cooked rice, cooled
2 eggs, scrambled
1 cup fresh bean sprouts
½ cup chopped fresh scallions
½ cup shredded lettuce
2 teaspoons soy sauce

Heat oil in a wok or heavy skillet over high heat. Add rice and stir-fry for about 5 minutes, or until rice is light brown. Mix in remaining ingredients and stir-fry to heat through. Serve immediately. *Serves 4 to 6.*

CRISPY SALAD

2 cups shredded kohlrabi
1 cup shredded sweet red pepper
½ cup bean sprouts
5 tablespoons soy sauce
1 tablespoon sesame oil
Dash of Chinese hot oil, optional
1 tablespoon rice wine vinegar
1 teaspoon sugar

Combine all ingredients together. Cover and refrigerate for 1 hour before serving. *Serves 4 to 6.*

CARAMEL CUSTARD

1½ cups sugar
6 eggs, beaten
3 teaspoons vanilla
4 cups milk, scalded

Preheat oven to 325°. Place 1 cup sugar in a heavy skillet over medium heat. Cook, stirring constantly, until sugar is golden. Do not brown. Pour melted sugar into a 2-quart casserole, turning to cover sides and bottom.

Beat the eggs, ½ cup sugar, and vanilla together. Slowly add warm milk, beating constantly. Pour into casserole.

Set in a pan of hot water and place in center of oven. Bake at 325° for 1 hour, or until knife inserted in center comes out clean.

Cool and refrigerate for at least 2 hours before serving. When ready to serve, invert casserole, and unmold. Spoon sugar syrup over top. *Serves 4 to 6.*

OTHER RECIPES

✿

BIGHORN WELLINGTON

1 Bighorn sheep loin roast, boned (about 3½ pounds)
2 cups rosé wine
¼ cup chopped mushrooms
¼ cup chopped parsley
1 teaspoon fresh tarragon leaves, crushed
  Salt and pepper to taste
1 clove garlic, crushed
1 recipe Plain Pastry (see page 8)
1 egg
2 tablespoons water
1 tablespoon cornstarch
¼ cup water
  Fresh tarragon or parsley, optional

Remove excess fat from roast. Mix together wine, mushrooms, parsley, tarragon, salt, pepper, and garlic. Pour over meat in large glass or ceramic bowl. Cover and refrigerate at least 8 hours.

Preheat oven to 325°. Remove meat from marinade. Strain marinade, reserving both wine and mushroom mixture. Spread mushroom mixture over meat and roll up evenly as for jelly roll. Tie at several points with heavy string. Place on rack in shallow baking pan. Insert meat thermometer so tip is in center of thickest part of meat.

Bake at 325° for 1½ hours or until meat thermometer registers 160°. Remove from oven and let stand 30 minutes. Remove string and pat dry with paper towel.

Increase oven temperature to 425°. Roll pastry into 12-inch square. Cut off a 2-inch strip from one side for design. Place roast in center of pastry. Bring up sides; seal seam and ends securely. Moisten with water if necessary. Place pastry-wrapped roast seam-side down in jelly roll pan or shallow baking dish. Roll out 2-inch strip of pastry; cut out small designs. Garnish top of pastry with cutouts. Mix egg and 2 tablespoons water; brush over top and sides of pastry.

Place reserved wine marinade in small saucepan over medium heat. Bring to a boil. Dissolve 1 tablespoon cornstarch in ¼ cup water and immediately whisk into boiling wine. Lower heat and cook until slightly thick. Remove from heat and keep warm.

Bake roast at 425° for about 30 minutes, or until pastry is golden brown. Place on platter and garnish with fresh tarragon or parsley. Serve wine sauce on the side. *Serves 6.*

TABASCO BOAR

2 *cups diced cooked boar*
3 *tablespoons vegetable oil*
1 *green pepper, seeded and chopped*
1 *large onion, chopped*
2 *stalks celery, diced*
2 *cups leftover gravy*
2 *tablespoons catsup or chili sauce*
½ *teaspoon ginger*
½ *teaspoon dry mustard*
   Few drops of Tabasco sauce
1 *tablespoon vinegar*

Heat vegetable oil in heavy skillet over medium heat. Sauté green pepper, onion, and celery until soft, but not brown. Add boar. Stir in gravy, catsup, ginger, mustard, Tabasco sauce, and vinegar. Simmer for 10 minutes. Serve over spaghetti, noodles, or rice. *Serves 4 to 6.*

ROAST FILLET OF BEAR

1 *whole fillet of bear*
3 *strips salt pork*
2 *green peppers, seeded and cut into strips*
½ *cup red wine vinegar*
2 *cups dry white wine*
¾ *cup sliced onions*
1 *clove garlic, minced*
1 *carrot, sliced*
1½ *cups chopped celery and leaves*
   Salt and pepper to taste
1 *bay leaf*
½ *teaspoon dried tarragon*
½ *cup melted butter*
2 *tablespoons butter*
12 *pitted black olives*
   Lemon slices
   Wine or currant jelly

Prepare the fillet by pulling out the veins and nerves. Pull strips of salt pork through it crosswise, then insert the green peppers.

In a saucepan over medium heat, combine vinegar, wine, onions, garlic, carrot, celery, salt, pepper, bay leaf, and tarragon. Bring to a boil and cook, over high heat, for 3 minutes. Remove from heat and cool. Place the meat in a glass or pottery bowl and pour the marinade over it. Cover and marinate, refrigerated, for 3 days, basting and turning occasionally.

Preheat oven to 450°. Drain the meat and place on a spit or in a roasting pan. Roast at 450° for 20 minutes. Brush with melted butter, reduce heat to 350°, and roast for 12 minutes per pound, basting frequently with melted butter.

Melt 2 tablespoons butter in a small skillet over low heat. Add olives and fry for 2 minutes. Transfer the meat to a hot platter and garnish with the olives, lemon slices, and wine or currant jelly. *Serves 6 to 8.*

SHERRY-BAKED LION

1 12- to 14-pound hickory-smoked rump roast of lion
8 whole cloves
8 black peppercorns
1 or 2 bay leaves
½ cup vinegar
1 stalk celery, diced
3 carrots, diced
1 large onion, chopped
   Whole cloves to "quilt" lion
2 cups brown sugar
1 cup sherry
1 apple for each serving

Scrub roast with a stiff brush and soak in water overnight. Place in a large kettle and cover with water. Bring to a boil, discard water, and cover with fresh water.

Add spices, vinegar, and vegetables; simmer slowly, allowing 25 minutes per pound, or cook until the smallbone of the lion feels loose. Cool in the stock.

Preheat oven to 350°. Remove the skin and place roast in a roasting pan. Score fat in a diamond pattern and stud with whole cloves. Pat on a coat of brown sugar ½ inch thick and spoon sherry over. Place cored apples around the roast. Bake in a moderate 350° oven for 30 minutes until well glazed. Baste both roast and apples several times with sherry drippings. *Serves 20 to 30.*

Chapter Six

SMALL GAME

MENU

❧

Garlic Hare with
Buttered Noodles

Green Beans Almondine

Raw Cranberry Salad

New York Cheesecake

GARLIC HARE

    2 *hares, cut into pieces*
 ¼ *cup white wine*
    2 *tablespoons minced garlic*
    1 *cup chicken stock*
       Salt to taste
 ½ *tablespoon flour*
 ¼ *teaspoon paprika (or more)*
1½ *cups heavy cream*
    1 *cup cooked sliced mushrooms*

Place hares in heavy saucepan over medium heat. Add wine, garlic, and stock; simmer about 1 hour, or until tender. Add salt when almost done. Blend flour and paprika, adding enough cream to make a smooth paste. Add remaining cream to hares. Gradually

249

stir in flour. Add mushrooms, stirring constantly, until thick. Add more seasonings if desired. Serve with buttered noodles. *Serves 4.*

GREEN BEANS ALMONDINE

1 pound steamed green beans
½ cup butter
¼ cup slivered almonds
  Salt and pepper to taste

Melt butter in heavy skillet over medium heat. Add almonds and sauté for about 10 minutes or until almonds are light brown. Stir in beans, add salt and pepper and serve immediately. *Serves 4.*

RAW CRANBERRY SALAD

1 package lemon Jell-O
1½ cups boiling water
¼ cup sugar
½ cup crushed pineapple, drained
½ cup finely chopped celery
1 apple, diced
½ orange, diced, including peel
  Juice and grated rind of ½ lemon
½ cup chopped nut meats
2 cups chopped lowbush cranberries
1 head lettuce, chopped

Pour boiling water over the lemon Jell-O. Add sugar and stir until dissolved. Set in refrigerator. When it begins to jell, stir in the remaining ingredients, except lettuce. Chill until set. When set, cut into serving portions and serve on a bed of chopped lettuce. *Serves 4 to 6.*

NEW YORK CHEESECAKE

2 *pounds cream cheese, softened*
1 *cup sugar*
6 *eggs*
1 *tablespoon flour*
1 *tablespoon vanilla extract (or any flavor you desire)*
2 *cups Zwieback crumbs*
½ *cup melted butter*
½ *teaspoon ground cinnamon*
¼ *cup sugar*
½ *cup sour cream, optional*
1 *tablespoon sugar, optional*

Preheat oven to 300°. Beat cream cheese and sugar until sugar has dissolved. Beat in eggs, one at a time, until well blended. Add flour and vanilla. Mix well. Set aside.

Mix together the crumbs, melted butter, cinnamon and sugar. When well mixed, press into the bottom and sides of a greased 9-inch springform pan. Pour in cream cheese mixture. Bake at 300° for 1 hour, or until cake is set. Remove from heat and cool, away from drafts. *Serves 8 to 10*.

OPTION: Blend sour cream and sugar, and coat top of cooled cake.

MENU

ᔔᔑ

Wild Rabbit Soup

Hungarian Melted Onions

Buttermilk Biscuits (see page 7)

Frozen Oranges

WILD RABBIT SOUP

1 rabbit, cut into small pieces
2 tablespoons flour
   Salt and pepper
⅓ cup vegetable oil
¼ cup chopped white turnip
½ cup chopped onion
½ cup chopped carrot
2 stalks celery, cut into pieces
¾ cup flour
4 quarts brown stock
1 bouquet garni
3 ounces rabbit or chicken blood
6 ounces port wine
1 tablespoon red currant jelly
   Salt and pepper to taste

Toss rabbit in flour, salt, and pepper. Heat oil in heavy skillet. When smoking hot, fry rabbit and vegetables until light brown. Add ¾ cup flour and cook to a golden brown. Add stock and bouquet garni and bring to a boil. Lower heat and simmer, skimming frequently, for 2½ hours, or until the flesh of the rabbit comes easily from the bones. Turn into a sieve and remove a few pieces of meat. Cut into ¼-inch cubes to be used for garnish. Rub remainder of meat and vegetables through the sieve. Return to heat. Add blood of the rabbit, wine, red currant jelly, and seasoning. Warm, but do not boil. Put the garnish into a hot soup tureen and pour the soup over. *Serves 6.*

HUNGARIAN MELTED ONIONS

½ cup butter
1 pound yellow onions, thinly sliced
6 hard-boiled eggs
¼ cup flour
2 cups milk, at room temperature
Salt and pepper to taste
Hungarian paprika
Fresh parsley for garnish

Melt butter in a heavy 3-quart Dutch oven over medium heat. Add onions and cook, stirring constantly, for 25 minutes, or until onions lose their shape and become quite clear. Do not brown them. Cut eggs into ½-inch-thick slices, and set aside.

When onions are cooked, gradually sprinkle in flour, stirring to mix well. Stirring constantly, blend in milk and cook until sauce boils and thickens. Season with salt and pepper to taste. Carefully add egg slices, leaving out a dozen or so for the top. Do not break up eggs. Spoon gently onto a heated, rimmed platter. Garnish with remaining egg slices and sprinkle with Hungarian paprika. Put sprigs of fresh parsley around the edge. Serve with buttermilk biscuits. *Serves 4 to 6.*

FROZEN ORANGES

3 *oranges*
1 *envelope unflavored gelatin*
½ *cup cold water*
1½ *cups fresh orange juice*
¼ *cup sugar*
1 *teaspoon grated orange rind*

Cut oranges in half. Scoop out pulp. Remove membrane and seeds, chop pulp, and drain off juice. Reserve orange halves, pulp, and orange juice.

In a small saucepan over low heat, sprinkle gelatin over cold water. Cook, stirring constantly, until gelatin is dissolved. Remove from heat. Add enough orange juice to reserved juice to make 1½ cups.

Stir in orange juice, pulp, sugar, and orange rind. Refrigerate for 1 hour or until very thick. When thick, beat until very soft. Fill orange halves and place in freezer. Freeze any remaining filling. When frozen, mound on top of frozen orange halves. Serve immediately as filling melts quickly. *Serves 4 to 6.*

OTHER RECIPES

❦

PECAN-STUFFED RABBIT

1 2-pound rabbit
1 clove garlic, halved
3 tablespoons butter or margarine
1 large onion, sliced
⅓ cup sliced celery
⅓ cup sliced fresh mushrooms
1½ cups cornbread stuffing mix
½ cup chopped pecans
¼ teaspoon sage
⅛ teaspoon pepper
2 cups boiling water
2 teaspoons instant chicken bouillon
4 medium carrots, sliced
¼ cup water
3 tablespoons flour
1 tablespoon chopped fresh parsley

Line a 12-by-9-by-2-inch baking pan with heavy duty aluminum foil, leaving 1½-inch foil collar. Rub cut edges of garlic over surface and cavity of rabbit. Wrap rabbit in foil and refrigerate 1 hour. Melt butter in small skillet over medium heat. Sauté half the onion slices, celery, and mushrooms until tender. Combine with stuffing mix, pecans, sage, and pepper. Dissolve bouillon in water. Mix ¼ cup into stuffing. Set aside remaining 1¾ cups.

Preheat oven to 350°. Fill cavity of rabbit with stuffing; secure flank skin. Place rabbit on its side in pan with remaining onion slices underneath and on top. Add carrots and remaining bouillon. Cover with foil. Bake at 350° for 1½ hours, or until meat is easily removed from bone. Carve and place on heated serving platter.

For gravy, strain broth from pan (about 1½ cups). In saucepan, stir water into flour until smooth; add broth. Bring to a boil, stirring until thick; add parsley. Serve with carved rabbit. *Serves 4 to 6.*

HASENPFEFFER

2 rabbits, cut up
1 recipe Wine Marinade
1½ cups diced onion
1 cup small or quartered mushrooms
4 slices bacon, cut up
3 tablespoons butter
Salt and pepper to taste
½ cup all-purpose flour
½ cup sour cream

Cover rabbits with Wine Marinade. Cover and refrigerate for 2 days.

In a large Dutch oven, over medium heat, sauté onions, mushrooms, and bacon until onions are soft. Lift out vegetables and bacon and reserve. Add 3 tablespoons butter to pan. Remove rabbit from marinade and pat dry. Strain marinade. Sprinkle salt and pepper over rabbit. Dip in flour and brown in butter, a few pieces at a time. When all rabbit is brown, return cooked pieces to pan. Add onion mixture and pour in strained marinade. Cover and simmer 1 hour or until tender. Place rabbit on a heated serving platter. Stir remaining flour into sour cream and add to sauce. When well blended, spoon over rabbit. *Serves 8.*

WINE MARINADE

2 cups wine
1 cup water
½ cup vinegar
1 tablespoon lemon juice
12 peppercorns
4 cloves garlic
½ teaspoon each dried thyme, rosemary, and marjoram
1 cup celery leaves

Mix all ingredients together. Use as a marinade for any game. *Makes approximately 4 cups.*

RABBIT PAPRIKA

1 3-pound rabbit, cut into serving pieces
2 tablespoons vegetable oil
1 medium onion, chopped
1 clove garlic, minced
2 small tomatoes, skinned, seeded, and chopped
½ cup seeded and chopped green peppers
1 to 2 tablespoons paprika (depending on pungency)
  Salt to taste
1 chicken bouillon cube
1 cup hot water
1 cup sour cream

Preheat oven to 350°. Heat oil in heavy skillet over medium heat. Add rabbit, onion, and garlic; sauté for about 20 minutes or until golden brown. Add tomatoes and green peppers. Mix paprika and salt and add to rabbit.

Dissolve bouillon cube in hot water and pour in. Place rabbit and sauce in a greased 2-quart casserole. Cover tightly and bake in a 350° oven for 1½ hours, or until tender. Remove rabbit pieces from the casserole and keep warm. Stir in sour cream and mix thoroughly. Spoon sauce over rabbit and serve immediately. *Serves 4.*

MENU

❦

Wild Willy's Raccoon Recipe

*Cauliflower
with Red Sauce*

*Tossed Green Salad
with Chef's Dressing (see page 172)*

Baked Peaches

WILD WILLY'S RACCOON RECIPE

*1 4- to 6-pound raccoon, skinned and cleaned
  Salt water (4 tablespoons salt per quart of water)
2 tablespoons baking soda
2 tablespoons butter
1 small onion, diced
2 stalks celery, chopped
1 teaspoon salt
1 teaspoon dried tarragon or basil
1 teaspoon tumeric
4 cups dried bread, cubed
2 tablespoons parsley, chopped
1 10-ounce can cream of chicken soup
  Milk, chicken stock, or melted butter, as needed*

258

Soak raccoon in salt water to cover overnight in the refrigerator. Remove from salt water and scrape off all fat, inside and out. Place raccoon in Dutch oven and cover with water. Bring to a boil over medium heat; lower heat and simmer for 45 minutes. Add the baking soda and continue to cook, uncovered, for 5 more minutes. Drain and wash in warm water. Put the meat in cold water and again bring to a boil. Simmer for 15 minutes. Remove from water and drain.

Preheat oven to 350°. Melt butter in a small skillet over medium heat. Add onion and celery and sauté until soft. Combine with remaining ingredients to make a bread stuffing. Add moisture using milk, chicken stock, and melted butter as needed; the dressing should be fairly dry. Stuff the raccoon with bread dressing and bake covered at 350° for 45 minutes. Uncover and bake for 15 additional minutes. Serve immediately. *Serves 4 to 6.*

NOTE: Allow 1 pound of meat per serving.

CAULIFLOWER WITH RED SAUCE

1 large head cauliflower
⅓ cup thick and chunky Mexican salsa (commercially available)
1 tablespoon crumbled queso, fresco, or feta cheese

Break cauliflower into flowerettes and steam until tender, about 12 minutes. Do not overcook. Arrange the cauliflower in a serving dish and top with the salsa.

Garnish with the crumbled cheese and serve. You may also place under broiler for a minute to melt cheese, if desired. *Serves 4 to 6.*

BAKED PEACHES

3 cups sliced fresh peaches
½ cup melted butter
½ cup light brown sugar
½ teaspoon ground cinnamon
½ cup bread crumbs
1 cup heavy cream

Preheat oven to 300°. Place peaches in buttered 1½-quart casserole. Mix butter, sugar, and cinnamon and pour over peaches. Sprinkle on bread crumbs. Bake at 300° for about 45 minutes or until peaches are bubbly and brown. Pour heavy cream over top and serve hot. *Serves 4 to 6.*

OTHER RECIPES

❀

SWEET COON PIECES

1 2- to 4-pound raccoon, skinned, cleaned, and cut into serving
  pieces
1 large onion, chopped
1 teaspoon salt
½ teaspoon pepper
1 teaspoon dry mustard
1 teaspoon allspice
1 cup catsup
4 cups beef broth
1 teaspoon ground ginger
½ cup vinegar
1 cup brown sugar

Preheat oven to 350°. Parboil the pieces of raccoon following instructions in Wild Willy's Raccoon Recipe (pages 258–59). Scrape off all fat. Place pieces in a roasting pan, add the onion and sprinkle with salt, pepper, mustard, and allspice.

In a saucepan over medium heat, mix the catsup, broth, ginger, vinegar, and brown sugar. Pour over raccoon pieces. Cover and roast at 350° for about 2½ hours or until tender. *Serves 2 to 4.*

NOTE: Allow 1 pound of meat per serving.

MENU

❧

Squirrel Stew, Georgia Style

Garlic Salad

Indian Corn Muffins (see page 37)

Cranberry Cobbler

SQUIRREL STEW, GEORGIA STYLE

2 *squirrels, cleaned and cut into 6 pieces each*
⅛ *pound salt pork, cut into small cubes*
2 *tablespoons flour*
¼ *teaspoon pepper*
  Salt to taste
2 *large onions, thinly sliced*
2 *cups beef broth*
  Leafy tops of 2 stalks celery
2 *cups fresh lima beans*
2 *large ripe tomatoes, peeled and chopped*
1 *cup fresh corn kernels*
1 *teaspoon Worcestershire sauce*
1 *to 2 tablespoons flour*
  Pork cracklings, for garnish

Preheat oven to 350°. Fry salt pork until very crisp over medium heat. Remove from the pan and reserve. Dredge squirrel meat in flour, salt, and pepper; sauté in hot fat. When nearly brown on all sides, add onions and cook until soft. Place meat in a 3-quart casserole, together with broth and celery tops. Cover and bake at 350° for 1 hour. Remove celery tops. Add lima beans, tomatoes, corn, and Worcestershire sauce. Cover and bake for 30 minutes or until vegetables are tender. Skim off excess fat and thicken gravy with flour mixed with ½ cup cold water. Correct seasoning. Serve hot from the casserole, garnished with crisp pork cracklings. *Serves 4.*

GARLIC SALAD

4 *cups torn mixed salad greens*
1 *cup garlic croutons*
½ *cup chopped red onion*
3 *garlic cloves, mashed*
1 *tablespoon chopped fresh chives*
½ *cup olive oil*
¼ *cup red wine vinegar*
  Salt and pepper to taste

Combine salad greens, croutons, and red onion. Whisk together garlic, chives, olive oil, vinegar, salt, and pepper. Pour over salad and toss to coat. Serve immediately. *Serves 4.*

CRANBERRY COBBLER

2 *cups whole cranberries*
1½ *cups sugar*
¾ *cup chopped pecans (or walnuts)*
½ *teaspoon ground cinnamon*
2 *eggs*
1 *cup flour*
¾ *cup melted butter*

Preheat oven to 325°. Place cranberries in a buttered 10-inch baking dish. Sprinkle with ½ cup sugar, nuts, and cinnamon. Set aside.

Beat eggs and 1 cup sugar until light yellow. Add flour and melted butter; beat until well blended. Pour batter over berries and nuts. Bake at 325° for 1 hour or until set and top is golden brown. Serve warm with vanilla ice cream, whipped cream, or Vanilla Custard (see page 152). *Serves 4 to 6.*

MENU

❧

Ranch Woodchuck

Nebraska Summer Corn

Health Salad

Oatmeal Cake

RANCH WOODCHUCK

 2 woodchucks, cut up
½ cup plus 1 tablespoon all-purpose flour
½ cup clarified butter
12 thin slices prosciutto
 6 1-ounce slices Monterey Jack cheese, cut in half
½ cup chopped shallots
 3 large cloves garlic, minced
½ pound mushrooms, sliced
½ cup dry white wine
 1 cup chicken broth
 1 teaspoon each chopped fresh thyme and oregano, or ½ teaspoon
    each dried
½ cup sherry
½ cup cream
   Salt and pepper to taste

Preheat oven to 375°. Dip meat in flour (reserving 1 table-spoon). Melt butter in heavy skillet over medium heat. Brown meat on all sides. Arrange in a buttered 13-by-9-by-2-inch baking dish. Top each piece of meat with 1 slice prosciutto and 1 cheese slice. Sauté shallots and garlic in skillet until soft. Add mushrooms, wine, broth, and herbs. Bring to a boil and cook 10 minutes. Blend in remaining 1 tablespoon flour and a small amount of sherry. Stir in remaining sherry and cream. Season with salt and pepper. Pour sauce over meat. Cover and bake, at 375° for 40 minutes or until tender. *Serves 6.*

NEBRASKA SUMMER CORN

2 *cups fresh corn kernels (about 5 ears)*
½ *cup melted butter*
2 *eggs*
1 *cup sour cream*
1 *cup diced Monterey Jack cheese*
½ *cup cornmeal*
1 *4-ounce can diced green chilies*
1½ *teaspoons salt*

Preheat oven to 350°. Generously butter a 2-quart casserole. Purée 1 cup corn with butter and eggs in blender or food processor. Mix remaining ingredients. Add puréed corn and blend well. Pour into prepared pan and bake at 350°, uncovered, for 50 to 60 minutes. *Serves 6.*

HEALTH SALAD

2 *cups Italian tomatoes, quartered*
1 *cup chopped and seeded green pepper*
1 *cup cubed Kirby cucumbers*
½ *cup chopped scallions*
¼ *cup mayonnaise*
2 *tablespoons wine vinegar*
2 *tablespoons yogurt*
  Salt and pepper to taste

Mix all ingredients together. Cover and refrigerate for 1 hour before serving. *Serves 6.*

OATMEAL CAKE

1 cup oats
1½ cups boiling water
½ cup butter
1½ cups brown sugar
1 cup white sugar
2 eggs
1½ cups flour
1 teaspoon ground cinnamon
1 teaspoon baking soda
6 tablespoons melted butter
1 cup chopped nut meats
¼ cup cream

Preheat oven to 350°. Cover oats with boiling water and let stand 20 minutes.

Cream butter, 1 cup brown sugar, and white sugar until light and fluffy. Add eggs, stir in oats, flour, cinnamon, and baking soda. When well mixed, pour into a greased and floured 13-by-9-by-2-inch pan. Bake at 350° for 30 minutes or until knife inserted in center comes out clean. Remove from oven. Mix together the melted butter, ½ cup brown sugar, nut meats, and cream. Spread on warm cake. Turn thermostat to broil and place cake under broiler for 3 to 6 minutes or until top is bubbly. *Serves 8 to 12.*

MENU
❧

Roast Possum

*Molly McDuggan's Creamed Onions
with Peanuts*

Caraway Slaw (see page 37)

Banana Pudding

ROAST POSSUM

1 winter possum, dressed
2 red pepper pods
1 teaspoon salt
¼ teaspoon black pepper
⅛ teaspoon sage
2 tablespoons lemon juice
4 large yams, peeled and quartered
¼ cup brown sugar
½ teaspoon cinnamon
⅛ teaspoon ginger

Place dressed possum in a kettle with pepper pods. Cover with cold water. Bring to a boil and simmer for 1 hour. Remove from pot and place on a rack in a Dutch oven or roasting pan. Add 1 cup water. Sprinkle with salt, pepper, sage, and lemon juice. Place yams around the roast. Combine sugar, cinnamon, and ginger; sprinkle on top of yams. Cover and cook over very low heat on top of stove, or in a 325° oven for 2 hours or until the meat is crisp and brown. Transfer possum and yams to a hot platter to serve. *Serves 4 to 6.*

NOTE: Porcupine, raccoon, muskrat, woodchuck, and even beaver are cooked by this same method.

MOLLY McDUGGAN'S CREAMED ONIONS WITH PEANUTS

16 whole pearl onions
 2 tablespoons butter
 2 tablespoons all-purpose flour
 ¼ teaspoon salt
 2 cups milk
 ¼ cup whole salted peanuts
 ½ cup buttered bread crumbs
 ¼ cup coarsely chopped salted peanuts

Preheat oven to 400°. Butter a 1-quart casserole. Cook onions in boiling salted water until tender. Drain. Melt butter over medium heat and stir in flour and salt. Add milk and cook over medium heat, stirring constantly, until smooth and slightly thick. Add whole peanuts. Place onions in prepared casserole and pour cream sauce over them. Top with buttered bread crumbs and chopped peanuts. Bake at 400° for 10 minutes or until top is brown and bubbly. *Serves 4 to 6.*

BANANA PUDDING

2 cups milk
1 cup heavy cream
¼ cup flour
1 cup sugar
3 eggs
1 teaspoon vanilla
1 tablespoon sweet butter
1 box vanilla wafers
3 large ripe bananas, sliced

Combine milk and cream in top half of double boiler over boiling water. Whisk in flour. When blended, add sugar and eggs. Cook, stirring constantly, for about 20 minutes or until thick. Remove from heat and stir in vanilla and butter. Set aside.

Lightly grease an 8-inch square baking pan. Cover bottom and sides with vanilla wafers. Cover with sliced bananas and pour in custard. Sprinkle top with any remaining wafer crumbs. Refrigerate for at least 2 hours before serving. *Serves 6 to 8.*

Chapter Seven

SMOKING

Smoking Game and Fish

Smoked food appeals to just about everyone, even those who have not acquired a taste for game and fish dishes prepared in other ways. There are many quality smokers on the market that will allow you to smoke foods all year around. Models that I have used are the Coleman smoker grill and Brinkmann smoker products.

Cooking Methods

There are two methods of smoking food: dry or moist smoking.

Moist smoking, an old Oriental process, is a recent addition to other types of outdoor cooking. Use wood chunks for the "smoke" part. Fill the pan with water, wine, sauce, or any other marinade for the "moist" part. There is no turning or basting and less shrinkage. By cooking with a moist smoke vapor, you will get the tastiest, juiciest meat possible.

Cooking Tips

1. Select a proper wood—Hardwoods such as hickory, walnut, oak, and Osage orange are best for smoking. The smoke is what gives smoke-cooked foods their unique flavor and color. Never use evergreens (pine, cedar, or fir) because the resin and pitch in these woods will discolor the food and give it a bad taste.

Use chunks of wood about the size of a tennis ball. Soak the wood in water for at least half an hour before using.

After 1½ to 2 hours of smoking, add additional wood for more smoke and a heavier smoked flavor.

2. Marinades and sauces—A variety of flavors can be transmitted to smoked food by liquids used in the pan or by marinades and sauces used during the final stages of cooking. Everyone seems to have their own favorites, which include fruit juices, soy sauce, teriyaki sauce, wine, beer, liquid smoke, mustard, and any number of spices.

Marinades are popular because they can turn less expensive (and less tender) cuts of meat into tasty entrées.

Beer adds flavor to fish, meat, and poultry. It penetrates the meat and tenderizes it. Used with a drip pan, it becomes a basting sauce that gives a rich, dark color to roasts.

Naturally brewed soy sauce enhances the natural taste of meats. It can be rubbed onto the meat before smoking or used as an ingredient for other sauces.

Sugar-based glazes, sauces, and marinades will burn faster and should be brushed on during the final stages of cooking.

Liquid smoke is an all-natural hickory flavoring made from the smoke of burning hickory wood and is often used as an ingredient in marinades. It does not add calories and makes food taste as if it has been smoking for hours. It is low in sodium. Add it to vegetables, sprinkle it on coals, or rub it directly on meats to flavor and help browning.

Use plastic, ceramic or glass containers for marinating. The acids in marinades can take on the flavor of metals. Stainless steel containers are also suitable.

SMOKED ELK JERKY

This delicacy/survival food is in a class by itself and is easy to make at home. Jerky is dried meat—not cooked, but dried, with low, slow heat.

Select the leanest cut of elk or game you can find, and chill it until almost frozen. Cut into strips a quarter of an inch wide with the grain. Remove all fat, as even a small amount can turn rancid and ruin the whole batch.

If it is going to be smoked, the meat does not have to be marinated, but a marinade both tenderizes and adds to the flavor of the finished product.

MARINADE FOR JERKY

2 tablespoons salt
1 teaspoon pepper
1 teaspoon garlic powder
1 teaspoon Worcestershire sauce
1 tablespoon vinegar
10 drops Tabasco sauce
1 tablespoon liquid smoke

Mix ingredients together with enough water to cover a single layer of meat strips in a glass baking dish; marinate, covered, overnight in the refrigerator, turning once or twice.

Drain meat and pat it dry on paper towels.

Arrange strips of meat on the lower rack of the smoker unit, or hang them from the upper rack with spring-type clothespins or paper clips unbent to form hooks. This latter operation is best done in the kitchen with the rack supported on something else so you have room to work. The strips should not touch each other. Set the loaded rack into the smoker.

Temperature control is important. Low range (140° to 150°) is plenty. Open top vent (charcoal unit only) to allow moisture to escape. Some smoke will go with it, but do not worry. It will take up to 10 hours to dry a batch of jerky. It is done when the strips are stiff but still slightly flexible.

Store, in airtight plastic bags or another airtight container, and refrigerate for up to 3 months.

SMOKED PHEASANT

1 or 2 dressed pheasants (with skin)
Beer (enough to cover)
Seasoned salt

Place pheasant in a large bowl or enameled pan (do not use metal) and cover with beer. Refrigerate in marinade for 18 to 24 hours. Remove birds from marinade, dry with paper towels, and sprinkle with seasoned salt. Place the beer marinade in water pan of the smoker with enough water to fill. Put birds on oiled rack, cover the smoker/cooker and cook for 5 to 6 hours.

SMOKED BLACK DUCK

1 or 2 dressed ducks (with skin)
½ cup sugar
¼ cup salt
Water to cover
Paprika
2 bay leaves, crushed

Place ducks in large pan. Mix sugar and salt with enough water to cover birds and pour over the ducks. Cover and refrigerate for 24 hours. Remove the ducks from marinade and allow them to air dry for 1 hour on a cookie sheet. Sprinkle with paprika. Fill smoker water pan with water. Add bay leaves. Place ducks on oiled rack and cover smoker. Smoke for 4 to 5 hours, or until done.

SMOKE COOKING CHART

Game	Method	Cooking Time
Small game: Birds, squirrel	Full grill ½ pan water	1–2 hours (charcoal)
	Wood	1–2 hours
	Charcoal	1–2 hours
	Gas	45 minutes–1½ hours Done when legs move easily in joints
Large game:	Full grill ½ pan water	
	Wood	2–4 hours
	Charcoal	3–4 hours
	Gas	2–3 hours

Fish:
  Small whole, fillets
  steaks
	Full grill
	½ pan water
	½ full charcoal
		2–4 hours

	Wood	2–4 hours
	Gas	2–3 hours
Whole, large	Full grill ½ pan water	
	Wood	1–2 hours
	Charcoal	2–3 hours
	Gas	½–1 hour Done when fish flakes easily

Chapter Eight

GENERAL TIPS

FISH

The taste of fresh fish is determined by its freshness and how it is handled from the moment it reaches the boat.

When playing out the fish, especially a large one, bring it into the boat as quickly as possible to eliminate unnecessary stress. The fish will taste better and, if you decide to release it, its chance of survival will be much greater. There are pros and cons on the effectiveness of using a livewell. I believe that they work best when the water is cold and you have just a few fish competing for oxygen. Belly-up fish do not stay fresh for long.

Using a stringer will increase your chance of keeping the catch alive until you dock. My first choice is a cooler filled with crushed ice mixed with a little rock salt. Fish can be placed on this ice mixture for up to twelve hours and still retain their freshness if you leave the drain valve open to drain off any excess water. Most fish bruise easily. When you get a large thrashing fish in the boat, have a hammer handle handy to kill the fish immediately.

Fish are not brought into the boat if you plan to release them. When releasing fish, take every precaution not to handle any more than necessary. For a toothy fish, hold it firmly behind the head area, remove the hook, and release. For other fish (such as bass) hold firmly by the lower lip and follow the same procedure. It is important that you not touch the gill or any eye area, or handle the body of the fish, as each time you do so you remove protective slime, which makes the fish prone to skin infection.

PREPARING FOR COOKING

Several methods can be used to prepare a catch for cooking, but I generally fillet fish. There are a number of filleting methods used, but I will discuss only the quickest and easiest techniques.

METHOD ONE: for flat fish, pan fish, bass, etc.

1. Lay fish on its side and place the knife blade under the pectoral fin and cut through to the backbone.
2. Turn the blade sideways and cut parallel to the backbone from the head to the tail. A sawing motion will help guide the blade.
3. Remove the rib section; then repeat with the second fillet.
4. To remove the skin hold it at the tail end and slide the knife blade parallel along between the flesh and skin. (Even a good fillet knife will have to be re-steeled after filleting three or four fish.)

METHOD TWO: for round, contoured fish such as walleye, perch, and cod.

1. Place whole fish upright with belly to the board. Slide the knife blade behind pectoral fin and make an incision from the top of the fish to the belly.

2. Make a long incision along the back using the backbone as a guide. Cut straight down through the tail area.

3. Turn the fish on its side and finish by cutting along the rib cage, making sure not to cut into the insides.

4. Lay the fillet flat and repeat process of removing the flesh from the skin.

METHOD THREE: for northern pike. This is perhaps one of the best tasting fresh water fish available, but many pass it by because of the "bones." This is a simple way to remove what is known as the "Y" bone.

1. Fillet and remove the skin as you would on any other fish.

2. Feel along the center of the fillet. You will find small protruding bones (known as the "Y" bone). Insert blade down the row of bones and gently push away the bones as you cut along the edge. Do the same on the opposite side of the row of bones.

3. Pull away the strip of flesh with bones from large fillet. Use the large fillet.

STORING FILLETS

Clean fillets with a damp paper towel. Do not run under water as it will soften the flesh. If not preparing the fish immediately, store, covered in the refrigerator, immersed in ice water for up to forty-eight hours. If large fillets are a bit slimy or if the fish was just killed prior to filleting, follow this tip: Rinse fillets with a little salt water to firm them up. Rinse with clean, cold water to remove the salt.

Other methods of preparation are:

Whole—a fish is cleaned, scaled and left whole. Used for stuffing or broiling (as in trout) or stuffing and baking larger fish (such as bass or walleye).

General Tips

GUIDE TO FISH COOKING TIMES

Pan Frying	Size	Cooking Time
Whole Fillets	Up to 1½ inches thick	2–5 minutes each side Approx. 2½–3 minutes per ½ inch of fish; turn and cook 1½–3 minutes
Deep Frying		
Fillets	¼–½ inch thick	3–4 minutes
Baking		
Whole Fillets Steak		10–15 minutes per pound or until fish flakes
Oven Frying		
Fillets	¼ inch ½ inch ¾ inch	9–10 minutes 10–11 minutes 11–12 minutes
Broiling		
Fillets Steaks	¼–¾ inch 1 inch	2 minutes per side 5 minutes on one side, 2½ minutes on second side
Steaming or Poaching		
Whole		10 minutes per inch

FISH SUBSTITUTION CHART

Type	Species Name	Average Calories 4-ounce serving
Large Fat (2 pounds and larger)	Salmon	
	Chinook	248
	Coho	224
	Sockeye	243
	Pink	222
	Chum	221
	Atlantic	219
	Lake Trout	221
	Brown Trout	226
	Carp	290
Small Fat (Up to 2 pounds)	Salmon (Kokanee)	160
	Rainbow Trout	120
	Brook Trout	114
Large Lean (2 pounds and larger)	Walleye	106
	Largemouth Bass	119
	Smallmouth Bass	116
	Northern Pike	101
	Musky	125
	White Bass	112
	Striped Bass	116
Small Lean (Up to 2 pounds)	Bluegill	101
	Yellow Perch	103
	Bullhead	135
	Crappie	106
	White Bass	109
	Bass	105

UPLAND BIRDS

Since most upland bird hunting takes place during the warmer fall weather, it is ill-advised to stuff birds in a rubberized game bag, then continue hunting. Since there is no ventilation, your catch will quickly spoil. I always field clean, then hang in a cool, dry place for about twenty-four hours before preparing for the freezer or table.

It is generally recommended to cook upland birds in a covered or moist environment. To prevent drying out or overcooking, keep the temperature low and cook in a covered roaster or wrap in aluminum foil, basting frequently.

The age of a bird will determine how long and what cooking method is used. A large bird does not always mean that it is an older bird. On an older bird the spurs will be more worn, and if you press on the breastbone, it will not be as pliable as on a younger bird.

If you enjoy white meat, then the grouse should be your first choice. The plump, white breast meat will delight even the most finicky eater.

A helpful hint: If, when you pick up the game bird, it is still alive (or if butchering chicken) place head first in a small 5-gallon plastic bucket with a hole precut in the center of the bottom. As the head protrudes, it can be quickly removed with the slice of a sharp knife. The bird will quickly bleed out and eliminate any mess. This method will produce a much better tasting bird.

To preserve freshness and flavor, ducks should be immediately field dressed with the feathers left on and hung in a cool, dry place to age for about forty-eight hours. If temperatures are fluctuating, I suggest you clean the ducks immediately.

Unless you know the daily eating habits of your catch, trim off the fat and skin the bird. Ducks often have a fishy flavor and aroma that will be eliminated by skinning and trimming. The exception to this rule is if the duck is to be roasted whole; then an oven bag works well.

Cooks frequently ask, "How do you kill the gamey flavor?" What you taste is greatly affected by how the bird is handled. Since we cannot control temperature changes due to weather conditions or effects of contaminants, it does not take long for game to spoil. If you detect a strong aroma coming from the kitchen, spoilage is the culprit. Discard the game; not even a super sauce will save it.

Duck, if handled and prepared correctly, has a wonderful rich flavor that will delight the most discerning palate.

My favorite methods of cooking duck are roasting whole or split, grilling, or frying. When grilling a duck, I fillet off the breast meat (similar to the method for filleting a fish) and cook the duck with the skin on.

GAME

When making the decision to shoot, be certain the result will be a quick, clean killing shot. This will eliminate undue stress, which affects the taste of the meat. An improperly placed shot will cause a metabolic reaction, increasing the flow of adrenaline throughout a deer, which results in additional pressure on the nervous system. When blood vessels constrict, redistributing the blood to muscle and flesh, the fuel is turned into energy, and lactic acid waste products accumulate in the meat. This will account for a stronger tasting meat.

Not enough attention is given to properly removing a deer from the woods. After the deer is cleaned out, do not drag the carcass through swamp water and other contaminating elements. Use a buddy to help carry the deer by tying all four feet and the head securely to a short pole. When you use this method, carry along an extra six-foot piece of orange cloth to drape over the deer for safety.

When cleaning out a deer in the field, it is important to wipe the cavity thoroughly with a damp cloth or a handful of grass. After you get the animal to your vehicle, repeat the wiping out process. Do not use a hose or excess water to wash out the cavity as it will break down the fiber of the meat.

Most red meat can be effectively frozen, airtight, for up to six months. Always double-wrap with freezer paper or have it commercially sealed to eliminate any air contamination. When the weather is cool (40°), deer can be hung for a day or two before processing. It can be hung for a longer period of time if the temperature is near freezing.

Much of the large game in this country is spoiled through transportation. If you are planning a hunt out West, do not depend on the weather; spend a few extra dollars and rent a refrigerated trailer. Deer, transported on the hood of a car in warm weather, will spoil in two to three hours. Keep the carcass away from warmer areas of the vehicle—wheel wells, hood, and exhaust. To keep off road dust and tar, and to maintain a good image of hunters, you might want to cover the deer with a cheesecloth bag.

When preparing venison or any other antlered big game, many cooks make the mistake of handling the cuts as if they were beef. Whereas beef fat helps produce a flavorful taste and is important as a tenderizer in the meat, venison fat should always be trimmed. If possible, trimming should be done in the field and always before freezing. The tallow feel or aftertaste is often attributed to cooking the meat with the fat on. The silverskin that is left on when freezing to insulate the meat from freezer burn must be trimmed off prior to cooking as it will act like an elastic bandage and make the venison tough and strong tasting.

Venison, because of its nutritional value and low fat and low cholesterol content, is now popular with nonhunters. One cup of venison has approximately 130 calories, compared to 340 for equal amounts of beef. To bring out the rich, full flavor of venison, serve it piping hot and medium rare; do not overcook. Unless grilling, when you can lard the meat, venison should be cooked in a moist environment.

One of the greatest rewards of a successful hunt is the preparation of my favorite "opening day tenderloin." Most hunters overlook this most delicious piece of meat in the deer. To extract and remove the tenderloin from the deer, follow these few easy steps.

1. Take your left hand and reach in the body cavity and feel along the backbone. These two long strips of muscle are the tenderloins. In a deer they are only about a foot long.
2. Slide your fingers in behind the muscle and begin to pull the meat away from the backbone area; it will pull away easily.
3. After you have an idea where each begins and ends, take a sharp knife with your right hand and cut through at the top of the tenderloin and begin pulling it out. Finish by cutting through the bottom and remove.

If a deer is properly tended in the field and prepared with care, it will not require heavy sauces or marinades. In fact, sauce should be used sparingly to accent the flavor of the dish, not overwhelm it. Marinades are only recommended if you use a tough cut of meat, or if the deer is a big swamp buck. To maximize the effect of the marinade, cover it and let set for at least 48 hours.

SMALL GAME

Small game has been the mainstay of the outdoorsman since this country was first settled because it is easy to hunt and generally accessible everywhere. Squirrel is always delicious, but especially so after they begin to feed on the white oak acorns and hickory nuts. To produce a dish that will be fork-tender, squirrel must be cooked slowly and in a moist environment. Before cooking, the animal must be skinned properly, not always an easy task.

A method that I recommend is this: Make an incision with a sharp knife all around the center of the body; then pull the skin up over the head and front legs with one hand while holding the back legs with the other hand. This is always done more easily when the animal is still warm. This same method may be used for rabbits.

Many hunters associate the flavor of rabbit with that of chicken, and, in fact, say that rabbit is one of their favorite dishes. Despite the popularity of hunting rabbits, they are not always safe to eat. Rabbits, in most parts of the United States, are prone to a disease called tularemia, which can be detected by white or yellow spots on the liver. The disease is found in about 5 percent of all rabbits, so check closely before preparation. If diseased rabbits are eaten, at the very least, you will become quite ill. Most small game should be eaten only after the first cold snap.

Other small fur-bearing animals (including raccoon, muskrat, and woodchuck) carry more body fat and must be prepared with more care. When cleaning a raccoon, trim off all body fat and remove the scent glands on the legs. Parboiling or slow cooking on a spit will rid raccoon of most remaining fat and will produce a delicious sweet meat.

INDEX

299

ABOUT THE AUTHOR

TIMOTHY MANION is the author of the best-selling (over 360,000 copies sold via direct mail) *Wild Game and Country Cooking* and host of the PBS TV series of the same name. His new nationally syndicated twenty-six-part series begins in June 1987. He is also host of the syndicated radio talk show "American Outdoors" and has been featured in *Outdoor Life*, among others. He is president of the Manion Outdoors Company, in Delafield, Wisconsin. In 1986 he founded the International Game and Fish Cooking Association, which sanctions and organizes the Taylor California Cellars World Championship Wild Game Cookoff, and local and state cookoffs in all fifty states.

The Book Club offers 7 x 35 binoculars good for a wide range of outdoor activities. For details on ordering, please write: Book Club, Member Services, P.O. Box 2033, Latham, N.Y. 12111.